Introduction to the books of

THE NEW TESTAMENT

SAINT **SHENOUDA**PRESS

Introduction to the books of

THE NEW TESTAMENT

By Fr Tadros Malaty

ST SHENOUDA PRESS
SYDNEY, AUSTRALIA
2021

Introduction to the books of the New Testament
By: Fr Tadros Malaty

ST SHENOUDA PRESS
8419 Putty Rd,
Putty, NSW, 2330
Sydney, Australia

www.stshenoudapress.com

ISBN 13: 978-0-6451394-9-5

Contents

Introduction to THE GOSPELS

IN THE INTRODUCTION TO THE GOSPELS, YOU WILL FIND

Introduction to the gospel

✳

About the author

✳

The gospel's audience

✳

How the gospel is arranged

✳

Main themes in the gospel

The gospel of
ST MATTHEW

INTORDUCTION

The Language of its Writing

Papias, the bishop of Hierapolis, said that in the year 118 A.D., Matthew wrote the teachings in the Hebrew tongue so that everyone could interpret it as he could. This was also mentioned by St. Irenaeus and the scholar Origen, as well as the two saints, Cyril of Jerusalem, and Epiphanius. The Historian Eusebius, narrated to us that St. Pentinus in his visit to India, found the gospel according to St. Matthew in Hebrew for the believers, of whom Bartholomew the apostle left for them.

ABOUT THE AUTHOR

The word "Matthew" means "God's gift." In Hebrew it is "Nathanael", and in Greek it is "Theodoras", which was translated into Arabic as "Tadros." It is as if God, through His calling to Matthew, satisfied his heart as a Godly gift and redirected his soul away from the love of money and tax collection, and towards His heart instead.

St. Matthew the Evangelist, who is one of the twelve disciples, was a tax collector. His name was that of a Levite, and his father's name was Alphaeus. The Lord Christ saw him sitting at the collection place, and He told him, "Follow Me, we stood up and followed Him" (Matthew 9:9, Mark 2:14, Luke 5:29). The tax collector left the collection place, which the Jews looked at with hatred, as it represented the Roman's tyrannical authority and sign of humiliation of people for the account of the colonised, exploited Roman. Our teacher, Luke the Evangelist, recorded the great banquet which the Levite did for the master in his house. He invited his previous friends who were also tax collectors and sinners in order to test the sweetness of following the Lord Christ (Luke 5:29). This affected the Jewish teachers, and they said to the disciples, "When the Pharisees saw this, they asked his disciples, "Why does your teacher eat with tax collectors and sinners?" On hearing this, Jesus said, "It is not the healthy who need a doctor, but the sick." (Matthew 9:11-12).

THE GOSPEL'S AUDIENCE

The Aim of this Gospel

St. Matthew wrote his gospel to the Jews who were, and still are awaiting for the Messiah, who will raise the kingdom that will rule over the world. The writer is Jewish and who was a disciple of the Lord Christ. As such, he wrote to his brethren, the Jews, to declare to them that the awaiting Messiah has come. He corrected the concept of the Kingdom for them, moving them away from the materialistic and timely thought of it, to the spiritual and Heavenly thought.

He repeated the word "the Son of David", to confirm that the "Messiah" is the king who came from the tribe of Judah to reign-- not on the same level with which they have reigned in the promised land, however, but it is a Heavenly Kingdom (Matthew 13:43, 25:34), (7:21 8:11, 16:28). Truly, the Jews waited eagerly for the coming of the Messiah, the saviour to rule, and our Lord did just that, but not in the materialistic way they had thought it to be.

This gospel also had an apologetic side to it about the Lord Christ. Its message didn't stop at the confirmation that all of the prophecies of the Old Testament were fulfilled, but it also defended against the Jewish provocation. Thus, it spoke clearly about His birth from a virgin and the angel who defended her before her fiancé. It also narrated in detail the story of the resurrection, and the bribe in which the Jews paid the soldiers. As such, it was called R.V.G. Tasker. This gospel made the early Christian's defence.

G.D.Kilpatrick saw that the gospel in its origin was written for a Liturgical aim, so that its chapters are to be read during the Christians' worship. The gospel was characterised as one of clarity, abbreviation, and has a balance in the language used. However, some say that such characteristics did not mean that this gospel was written for this aim, but that they are the characteristics of the literacy of the writer and because of these characteristics, he used the gospel for Liturgical purposes.

Time and Place of Writing

Most students thought that it was written a few years after the gospel according to St. Mark, but before the destruction of the Jewish altar, as it talked about it as a prophecy and not as reality. Therefore, they estimate his writings to be within the third quarter of the first century.

Tradition says that the gospel was written in Palestine, a note by which none of the first fathers of the church doubt. However, some researchers believe that it was written in Antioch or Phenicia.

HOW THE GOSPEL IS ARRANGED

The Special Numbers within the Gospel

The evangelist Matthew cared about numbers that the Jews liked, especially the numbers 3, 5, and 7. Regarding the number 3, we find that he divided the descendants of the Lord Christ into three stages (1:17). He also mentions the three temptations that the Lord faced (4:1-11), and the three pillars of worship (6:1-18). He offered three metaphors for prayer: seeking, asking and knocking (7:7-8). In the transfiguration, the Lord took with Him three disciples (17:1); In Gethsemane (26:37), there He prayed three times (26:39-44), and St. Peter the apostle denied the Lord three times (26:75). We will try to speak about the meaning of numbers during our talk in explaining the gospel.

One of the most important features of this gospel, is that it consists of 5 large sections, which some suggest the gospel does in order to represent Christ as the new Moses, because of the five books from the Old Testament that Moses wrote.

The five sections of this gospel are:

1. The sermon on the Mountain

2. The apostolic work

3. The parables of the Kingdom

4. Various teachings

5. Talks about Eternity

THE MAIN CONTENT OF THE GOSPEL

1. The Descendants of the King and His birth, chapters 1-2

Matthew the evangelist confirmed through the descendants of the Lord Christ, according to the Jewish Law, that He is the Son of David from the tribe of Judas--the last King from the kingly tribe. He writes that with His coming, the records of descendants ended, as its purpose was fulfilled and it is now impossible for a Jewish person to know his descendants until Adam, as it was at the days of the Lord Christ.

2. The Preceding to the King, chapter 3

In the Eastern tradition, there had to be a person who preceded the king to prepare the way for him. Thus, the angel, John the Baptist, came to prepare the way for the Heavenly King.

3. The Testing of the King, chapter 4:1-11

The entrance of the Lord in a war with the devil on the mountain to grant His people the spirit of victory.

4. The Declaration of the King, chapter 4:12-25

He declared His Heavenly Kingdom which was on Earth.

5. The Constitution of the King, chapters 5-7

"The sermon on the mountain" is the constitution which people live by, to prepare them for Heavenly Life and to enjoy the Kingdom.

6. The Service of the King, chapters 8-11:19

As He declared His constitution to His people, He practiced His service with the needy, starting with the cleansing of the leper, touching him to confirm that He came for the sake of the outcasts and that the leper cannot defile the Lord. He then cured the servant of the centurion to declare that He came mostly for the sake of the servants and slaves, and not to despise a person for one reason or another.

7. The Rejection of the King, chapters 11-20

The Jews were disappointed in the Lord Christ, as they were waiting for a King with the idea that they will dominate and reign over all, creating a Zionist state over the world. His service differed from their idea, which was to open the door for the nations.

8. The Entrance of the King, chapters 21-25

His official entry into the capital was to reign on the Cross, after revealing the evangelical idea of the Kingdom.

9. The Death of the King and His Resurrection, chapters 26-28

The Lord reigned through the Cross, and resurrected to also resurrect the believers, who are members in His Heavenly Kingdom.

MAIN THEMES IN THE GOSPEL OF ST. MATTHEW

Special Features of the Gospel

This gospel is used in the writings of the first church, more than the others. Perhaps its publication for the sermon over the mount in a detailed way, as a constitution for the Christian life, had its effect on the believers.

The Relationship between Christianity and the Old Testament

Seeing as Matthew the Evangelist wrote this gospel for the Jews, he revealed in a deep way the confirmed relationship between Christianity and the Old Testament. He clarified how the church was full of thoughts of the prophecies of the Old Testament, which were fulfilled spiritually in Christ Jesus our Lord. It pointed out around 60 prophecies from the Old Testament, and the word Kingdom was repeated approximately 55 times. Also, the Lord Christ as Son of David was mentioned eight times, declaring that He is the promised one. This gospel held onto the Jewish atmosphere more than the other gospels. It assumes that the reader knew Hebrew (19:5), as he used favourite expressions to the Jews, such as calling Jerusalem the holy city (4:5, 27:52-53) and the altar with the holy place (15:24). He spoke about the foundations of the three good deeds for the Jews, being giving, prayer and fasting (6:1, 16-18), as well as the duties of the priests in the altar (12:5), the tax of the altar (17:24-27), the tenth (23:23), and the washing of the hands as a sign of being clean from blood (27:24) etc.

Matthew clarified that the Lord didn't come to look down on the Old Testament, but to fulfil its purpose of perfection through Law and Commandments, fulfilling the promises of salvation. This fulfilment wasn't accomplished only through doctrines of the Lord Christ, but also through His Person as a Saviour and Redeemer. This is what pushed some of the scholars to start looking to this gospel as a Christian study to reveal the declaration of the hidden Lord Christ in the Old Testament.

Matthew the evangelist wrote to the Jews, and didn't shy away from speaking honestly about their mistakes. He says about the Roman centurion, "When Jesus heard this, he was amazed and said to those following him, "Truly I tell you, I have not found anyone in Israel with such great faith. 11 I say to you that many will come from the east and the west, and will take their places at the feast with Abraham, Isaac and Jacob in the kingdom of heaven. 12 But the subjects of the kingdom will be thrown outside, into the darkness, where there will be weeping and gnashing of teeth." (Matthew 8:10-12).

He also writes, "the Son of Man will be delivered over to the chief priests and the teachers of the law. They will condemn him to death." (Matthew 20:18); "Therefore I tell you that the kingdom of God will be taken away from you and given to a people who will produce its fruit." (Matthew 21:43); "At that time Jesus went through the grain fields on the Sabbath." (Matthew 12:1); They took attention to their outward appearances, (6:2, 5, 16); They were after some of the traditions which are against the commandment (15:3-9); He confirmed their abidance to the Law commandments and His severe criticism to opinions the Scribes and Pharisees.

Although this gospel was written in a way that addressed the Jews more than the other gospels, it still did not neglect the uneducated reader. He does this by explaining some of the known Jewish words, such as "Immanuel" (which means "God with us") (Matthew 1:23) and "Golgotha" (which means "the place of the skull") (Matthew 27:33). He also explained some of the geographical sides to it, as he writes, "Leaving Nazareth, he went and lived in Capernaum, which was by the lake in the area of Zebulun and Naphtali." (Matthew 4:13), as well as explaining beliefs and habits that a Jew would know, such as, "That same day the Sadducees, who say there is no resurrection." (Matthew 22:23), and "Now it was the governor's custom at the festival to release a prisoner chosen by the crowd." (Matthew 27:15).

The evangelist addressed Jewish matters not only by using the prophecies of the Old Testament, but also through abiding by the Commandments Law (5:8), and the teaching of both the Scribes and the Pharisees who were sitting on Moses' chair (23:2) in a deep and new spiritual way. The master declared that He was sent for the Jewish lost sheep (15:24) and that His descendants belong to Abraham, the father of the Jews, as well as that it is divided into three divisions, which are composed of 14 ages. He was the awaiting Son of David who entered the holy city as a winner. These all point to the fulfilment of Jewish wishes. However, the evangelist didn't stop at this, also noting the Jewish thoughts to gather the evangelist message, revealing the new Jewish appearance that does not stop at the narrow border. It came to the descendants of the Lord, an uneducated strange race, where in His childhood He had escaped to Egypt for shelter, declaring the embracement of the gentiles into His Kingdom (2:13). In His meeting with some of the uneducated, He praised them, revealing their strong faith, whilst also attacking the Scribes and the Pharisees in their hypocrisy and small mindedness. In the parable of the vinedresser, He spoke about the surrender of the vine to another vinedresser (21:33). It is as if He moved them from narrow fanatic understanding, to the spiritual, new understanding and declaration of the great message, which is extended to all gentiles, as he ended the gospel with the words of the farewell words of the Lord, "Therefore go and make disciples of all nations." (28:19).

The Divine Elements of the Gospel

Matthew's Gospel is the "Gospel of Kingdom" or the "Heavenly Kingdom", which is clearly revealed in the teachings and talks of the Lord Christ, shown through His parables and miracles. This Kingdom is the future Kingdom (25:34, 7:21, 8:11, 16:28), but it starts from now in our lives as a present truth (12:28, 4:17, 5:13, 11:3). It is as if the Heavenly Kingdom began truly by the coming of the Lord Christ and His dwelling in our hearts, which will be completed at His last coming.

The Lord of the Kingdom (The Messiah), is the Saviour by which the Holy Bible reveals His Royal authority, clarifying that in Him, the written was accomplished, and the Divine promises are fulfilled. We see this by the new Moses, who, on a high and unique level, fasted 40 days. He was to be tested on the mount to have victory in the name of His people, and the angels served Him, to accomplish Moses' Law not by receiving commandments on a carved stone, but to speak in an authority by Him, satisfying the people which are in the Wasteland. He was transfigured before His disciples, calling Moses and Elijah who He spoke to them with!

He is the Son of God, but He is also the Son of Man, as He was amongst us to bring us into His glory. Therefore, Matthew called Him "The Son of Man" to truly glorify Him.

The Church Elements of the Gospel

As the gospel of Matthew the evangelist was the gospel of the Kingdom, it is also called "the Gospel of the Church", as it is the mystery of God's Kingdom. It is unique amongst the evangelists, which recorded to us special teachings of the church, as it has a frank and clear way of speaking on the Lord Christ. Matthew attributed to Jesus the word "ecclesiastically" twice, in two sentences, which were very important. He spoke about the base of the Church, the rock of faith, saying to Peter the apostle when he declared his faith in Him, "and on this rock I will build my church, and the gates of Hades will not overcome it." (Matthew 16:18).

He also spoke about the authority of the church, writing, "But if they will not listen, take one or two others along, so that 'every matter may be established by the testimony of two or three witnesses.' 17 If they still refuse to listen, tell it to the church; and if they refuse to listen even to the church, treat them as you would a pagan or a tax collector. 18 "Truly I tell you, whatever you bind on earth will be bound in heaven, and whatever you loose on earth will be loosed in heaven." (Matthew 18:16-18).

This reveals to us the care that the evangelist Matthew has for Church's matters. We notice that he confirms the mystery of the Church like the presence of God amongst His people, and in their hearts, throughout the whole book. He opened the book with the angel talking to Joseph about the Lord Christ, saying that "they will call him Immanuel" (which means "God with us") (Matthew 1:23). He passed onto us the talk of the Lord with His disciples, introducing to us a simple image to the local church, through Christ saying, "For where two or three gather in my name, there am I with them" (Matthew 18:20). The Lord also revealed the hidden church in the heart of the one who testified for the truth, specially through his apostolic work. We see this when we writes, "Anyone who welcomes you welcomes me" (Matthew 10:40), and "And whoever welcomes one such child in my name welcomes me." (Matthew 18:5).

He manifested His presence amongst His suffering people, by saying on the last day, "whatever you did for one of the least of these brothers and sisters of mine, you did for me'" (Matthew 25:40).

The scholar Tertullian, thinks that the evangelist Matthew in his mentioning for the meeting of the Lord with His disciples inside the boat amongst the severe winds, was a living image of the church, who receives her peace from the Lord Christ who dwells within her, transfiguring inside in spite of the disturbances and harassment of the devil.

Finally, the evangelist ended the book with words of the Lord to His disciples, "Therefore go and make disciples of all nations, baptizing them in the name of the Father and of the Son and of the Holy Spirit, 20 and teaching them to obey everything I have commanded you" (Matthew 28:19-20). This was confirming that He will be with them all the days till the end of ages. It is as if the church now extends to all nations, waiting until His last coming to live with Him face to face!

The Eternal Elements of the Gospel

It is the book of the Heavenly Kingdom, which writes about the first coming of the Lord Christ to prepare the church to meet Him in His last coming (eternal) in chapters 24 and 25. In the first chapter, he spoke about the manifestations of the end of ages, not only for knowledge, but for the purposes of preparation, encouraging us to continuously watch for His last coming. In the following chapter, he offered a wonderful parable about the Heavenly Kingdom and our meeting with the Lord on the cloud.

The gospel of
ST MARK

INTRODUCTION

In our study of the Gospel according to St. Matthew, we experienced the joyful tidings of our Lord Jesus Christ. It is a gospel that God has provided through His saintly prophets so that we may receive it and be guided by it to enter His eternal Kingdom. As is in the gospel of St. Matthew, so also is in the gospel of St. Mark who shares the good news with us, however, from another perspective. In this particular gospel, we view our Lord Jesus Christ suffering on our behalf during His ministry, which we especially see in His acceptance of the passion, suffering, and crucifixion.

This gospel was written to the Romans, who were heavily dependent upon human strength as well as contemporary authority, which is mostly founded on violent tendencies. In this gospel, however, we are introduced to Christ as a true authority through His love and humility. Its aim is for us to experience being guided by the Spirit of our King through strength in suffering, love, and passion.

To preface before continuing your reading of this introduction to the gospel of St. Mark, I encourage you to first read through our interpretation of "The Gospel of St. Matthew." This is because much of Jesus' life and works are repeated across both gospels, with our previous contemplation making many references and quotes to the Church Fathers. For the purposes of avoiding repetition, it is best to read over it before continuing here.

ABOUT THE AUTHOR

The Gospel of St. Mark and St. Peter the Apostle

Certain scholars attempted to credit the gospel of St. Mark to the Apostle Peter, suggesting that St. Mark was just a scribe or interpreter for his relative, St. Peter. It was believed that the gospel is made up of memoirs of St. Peter's sermons to which St. Mark attended whilst with him in Rome, later transcribing it after the martyrdom of St. Peter and St Paul.

This perspective, however, has been completely rejected by the Orthodox Church. His Holiness, Pope Shenouda III, presented a study on "Saint Mark the Apostle " on the sixteenth century anniversary of his martyrdom. Whilst I encourage you to read the book and review it further in your own time, here are a few of the main points from His Holiness' study:

1. The concept that St. Mark only followed St. Peter to record the gospel is based on Papia's claim that St. Mark had never heard, nor met Jesus Christ, but accepted Him anyway. This view, as adopted by certain scholars, is incorrect, which is confirmed by several Church Fathers who studied the history of the church and in fact, confirmed the opposite view.

2. St. Mark was neither a scribe nor an interpreter for St. Peter during his ministry in Rome, as claimed by some. It was not St. Peter, but actually St. Paul who ministered there. In his epistle to the Romans, St. Paul clearly expresses his desire to work among them (Rom. 1:10- 11) and confirms his refusal to build on another man's foundation (Rom. 15:20). St. Paul was the preacher for the Gentiles, while St. Peter was a preacher for the Jews.

3. If St. Mark was merely a recorder of St. Peter's memoirs or sermons after his martyrdom, there would be no need to hide it. St. Mark would have certainly mentioned it as a matter of honesty and humility.

4. Some scholars base their claim on the fact that the gospel was written by St. Peter because it includes his own weaknesses, yet ignores his glories, which was done so out of modesty. This can be easily disputed, however, by the following sub-arguments:

a) The writers of the gospels are above personal levels in their task. We see this in the prophet Moses, for example, who identifies both his own strengths and weaknesses, such as, "The man Moses was very humble, more than all men who were on the face of the earth" (Num. 12:3). Moses' humility did not prevent him from mentioning the miracles that God did through him, how God appeared and spoke to him, accepted his intercessions, and complimented him. As well as weaknesses like how he was slow of speech and slow of tongue (Exod. 4:10), and his trespass that compelled God to forbid him from entering the promised land, "...Holy men of God spoke as they were moved by the Holy Spirit." (2 Pet. 1:21). In the New Testament, St. John the Beloved mentioned how he stood by the cross, how the Lord addressed him and put His mother in his care (Jn. 19:25-27), calling himself "the disciple, whom Jesus loved" and who "was leaning on Jesus' bosom" (Jn. 13: 3-25). Thus, avoiding self-glory is not strong enough to suggest that this is the reason why it was written by St. Peter and not St. Mark

b) St. Mark did not refrain from complimenting St. Peter the Apostle. He mentions the Lord's call for St. Peter as one of the first of its kind (1:16-20), putting his name ahead of all the other apostles (3:16) and placed the story of Christ entering his house to heal his mother-in-law as the first of the Lord's miracles in his gospel (1:29-31). He had also mentioned St. Peter's words to the Lord, "See, we have left all and followed you" (10:28), and his presence on several occasions together with James and John (5:37; 9:2-8; 14:32).

5. Other scholars centre their position around the fact that it mentions incidents that must have been experienced by an eyewitness, thus attributing its likelihood to St. Peter himself. However, if we consider St. Mark's calling from the Lord to be one of the seventy disciples and his mother's position among the followers of the Lord, we realise that several of these incidents were either witness by St. Mark himself, other disciples, his mother, or any one of those within the Lord's company.

THE GOSPEL'S AUDIENCE

St. Mark writing to the Romans

St. Mark had many interesting features throughout his gospel to the Romans. We have good reason to support the fact that he wrote especially to them due to his interest in language and translations. For example, he translates Aramaic expressions unknown to the Romans, such as "Boanerges" (3:17); "Talitha" (5:41), "Corban" (7:11), "Ephphatha" (7:34), "Eloi, Eloi, lama sabachthani" (15:34), and "Golgotha" (15:21). Had this gospel been directed to specifically the Jews, there would be no need to translate the meanings of these words, as they were well known to them.

Moreover, he explained Jewish customs, location, sects, and other things that were known to the Jews but unknown to the Romans. He elaborated on the concept of defilement of the Pharisees and the importance of washing things outside (7:2-4), the custom of killing the Passover lamb on the first day of Unleavened Bread (14:12), the meaning of the expression "the preparation day" (15:42), and the denial of the Sadducees about the Resurrection (12:18), etc. He mentioned the Jordan followed by the word "river," explained that the Mount of Olives is opposite the temple (13:3), and that Bethpage and Bethany are close to Jerusalem (1:11). All of this being information the Jews would presumably have known, but the Romans would not.

Unlike St. Matthew who was writing to the Jews, St. Mark avoided making many references to the Old Testament the way St. Matthew had, which again, works as a testament to his writing to the Romans. Keeping in mind that St. Mark was not writing to the Jews who are of religious nature, nor the Greeks who were people of philosophy and thought, but to the Romans, who were known as people of action, he provided them with a book small in size and with no introduction. As such, his main presentation of Jesus Christ was through his deeds or actions, and not by His sermons and speeches.

Time and Place of Writing

All scholars agree that the Gospel according to Mark is the oldest of all gospels. Many of them also believe it to be the main source from which the evangelists, Matthew and Luke, based their own gospels on. St. Irenaeus believes it to be written after the martyrdom of St. Peter and St. Paul, which is roughly after the year 67 A.D., with most scholars agreeing that it was likely between the years 65 and 70 A.D. According to St. John Chrysostom, this gospel was written in Egypt, but other scholars claim it was written in Rome.

HOW THE GOSPEL IS ARRANGED

The Messianic Secret of Jesus Christ

Keeping the Messianic Secret of Jesus Christ was how the foundation for the structure of the gospel was developed. The attention of some scholars was drawn to the fact that St. Mark the Evangelist expressed his opinion that the Lord Christ wished for His identity as the Son of God, to remain a secret not to be revealed until His Resurrection. This analysis, by W. Wrede, of the Gospel of St. Mark was based on four main points; The Lord abstained from revealing His secret as the Christ during His ministry on earth. He did, however, reveal that secret not to the multitude, but to His disciples, who were not able to comprehend it. The demons recognised Him, but He rebuked them and did not let them testify to Him. Moreover, as many of His miracles of healing that he performed revealed the Messianic Secret, He often ordered those He healed to refrain from proclaiming it.

Another scholar was convinced that St. Mark underlines the secret of the identity of the nature of the Lord Christ as He wished for it to be, based on the following reasons:

1. When the demons recognized Him, He forbade them from revealing His identity (1:25,34; 3:12).

2. The Lord Christ avoided the proclamation of His miracles and healings (1:44; 5:43; 7:36; 8:26), however, made an exception for Gentiles or those He healed that lived among Gentiles (5:19, 20).

3. The tendency of the Lord to withdraw from people (1:35; 3:7; 4:35; 6:31; 7:24; 8:27; 9:30).

4. His refusal of giving a sign to that generation (8:21).

5. More than once, He presented a clear teaching to His disciples when they were alone (4:33-34; 7:17-23; 9:28-31), but the parables He gave to the multitude seemed mysterious and incomprehensible to them (4:10-13).

6. The multitudes did not comprehend His parables because of the hard-heartedness of the Jewish people, or at least, of their leaders (3:5; 7:6, 7).

7. The Lord Christ refused to reveal His nature until the Son of God was raised from the dead (8:30; 9:9).

Hiding His nature seems to have been founded on the idea that the Lord Christ, with His true authority, did not seek worldly glory and so acted in humility. This was done so that when He rose from the dead, He would reveal His nature not to glorify Himself, but rather to glorify those who believe in Him so they could enjoy the power of His Resurrection.

Another perspective, however, offers the idea that hiding His nature may have been done in order to fulfil His divine purpose with the crucifixion. St. Paul the Apostle says that "had they (the Jews) known, they would not have crucified the Lord of glory" (1 Cor. 2:8).

MAIN THEMES IN THE GOSPEL OF ST. MARK

Special Features

The early Christians understood the word "gospel" to mean "good news for the world." We have looked into the significance of this word further during our previous study of the Gospel of St. Matthew, which I again encourage you to read over.

The word, "Gospel"

St. Mark, according to majority of scholars, was the first to use this expression as an attachment to a specific book, which presents the life of Jesus Christ as good news for the world. It seems as though St. Mark was particularly fond of this word, and included it within the first verse of his gospel, which says, "The beginning of the gospel of Jesus Christ, the Son of God." (Mk. 1:1). He uses it often throughout the book during several other occasions. For example, when writing on Jesus carrying the cross, he mentions the Lord saying, "Whoever loses his life for my sake and the gospel's, will save it" (Mk. 8:35). It is also worth mentioning that the word 'gospel" was not used by the evangelists, Matthew and Luke, during this particular situation (Mt. 16: 25; Lk. 9: 24). The same can be noted when Jesus said, "There is no one who has left house or brothers or sisters or father or mother or wife or children or lands, for my sake and the gospel's, who shall not receive a hundredfold now in this time... and in the age to come, eternal life." (Mk. 10:29) Again, St. Matthew did not mention the expression "gospel" in this instance. (Mt. 19:29).

St. Mark also included the word "gospel" in 1:14 and 15:14-9, as he preached among the pagan Gentiles and philosophers. The use of this word was especially joyful to him whilst in Alexandria, where he revealed the gospel of the Lord Jesus Christ and His offering as a sacrifice on the cross--a symbol of reconciliation between God and His people.

Power by Love and Passion, not Violence

As mentioned before, the Romans were people who believed in, and valued power and authority, having been rulers of the world at that time. It is for this reason that we see St. Mark presents our Lord Christ as a Man of real authority--a theme that is very apparent throughout the entirety of this gospel. Christ's authority is made evident upon His encounter with unclean spirits, (3); ailments (1); nature (4); plants (11); within the temple (11); and upon the Sabbath, as "the Lord of the Sabbath" (2). By His true authority, He was aware of secret thoughts (2) and revealed the secrets of the future (13). By His authority, He could feed the multitude (6:33-44; 8:1-9).

Whilst the Romans believed in authority obtained through violence, pride, and oppression, St. Mark the Evangelist aimed to proclaim the authority of the Lord by just the opposite: through humility and ministry to others (9:33; 10:35, 45). The concept of the passion and the cross prevailed throughout his whole book--almost of it--although, the book as a whole works as preparation for the soul to receive Christ our King through passion!

St. Mark the Evangelist presented Herod as an example of their kings, characterized by violence and murder, and around whom gathered those who seek fun and dance. At the same time, he presents the Lord Christ, who reigns by the gospel of the Kingdom, attracting and fulfilling the soul. The Evangelist often proclaims how multitudes gathered together around the Lord (1:28, 33, 45; 2:1, 2; 3:7-9; 4:1-2; 6:32-34; 7:24; 9:15; 5:24), and all ran after Him, even when He tried to retreat to a deserted place (6: 32-34) or to a certain house (7:24). Many times, the Evangelist proclaims how the multitudes were astonished at His teachings (1:22, 27; 4:41; 6:51; 10:24, 26). He never imposed Himself onto others the way the Romans were used to doing, but instead it was through His love and humility that He attracted the hearts of many.

Interestingly, throughout the gospel of St. Mark we find that he concentrates especially on the conflict and rejection our Lord experienced with the Jews, likely as an attempt to encourage the Romans to accept Him. Despite this, St. Mark does not fail to underline the fact that Christ did not show weakness whilst in the face of adversaries but was always able to expose their hypocrisy. In the face of His crucifixion, even, it is not revealed as a sign of His weakness, as the gospel reveals that our Lord foretold three times to His disciples that He would be crucified (8:31; 10:33,34) and would rise from the dead and come again in the glory of His Father, accompanied by the holy angels (8: 38) on the clouds of heaven (14:62).

Jesus loves the Gentles

In addition to these things, St. Mark particularly emphasised the Lord's approach toward the Gentiles (7:24-30; 11:17; 13:10; 16:15), ensuring to stress the value He placed on them. His last commandment was to "Go into all the world and preach the gospel to every creature" (16:15).

As the Evangelist addressed his gospel to the Romans, he stressed its Catholic nature for the purposes of encompassing the Gentiles as well, which is why he often uses the expressions of "whole" and "all" (1:5, 28, 33, 39; 2:13; 4:1; 6:33, 39, 41, 55; 13:10). A certain scholar also notes this, saying that "it is evident that St. Mark used to live among a Christian community of a Gentile origin, yet it was not completely isolated from Judaism, although it had its own blossoming culture."

Faith and Suffering

If the word "gospel" had been a favourite of St. Mark's, the word faith was the way to enjoy the worldly and spiritual blessings that the gospel offered. This book strongly emphasises that it is a lack of faith that keeps people from recognising the work of the Lord Christ (6:1-6). Certain scholars see that the Lord Christ is presented in this book as someone who dedicated His life to awaken the faith of man.

The purpose of this book is to prepare the soul in receiving the gospel of the Suffering Christ, which is why many of the sayings of the Lord in the gospel of St. Mark focuses on suffering as a whole. He spoke clearly and blatantly about most of Christ's sufferings on three occasions:

1. In 'Caesarea Philippi' (8: 31)

2. Passing through Galilee (9:30, 31)

3. On His way to the holy city (10: 33, 34)

Across these occasions, Jesus was either met with rebuke, as was done by Simon Peter who refused to accept this as our Lord's reality, or by fear and misunderstanding by all of the disciples. The mystery of the Cross was not yet recognised, although Jesus had prepared them for it previously on more than one occasion (see 2:20; 3:6; 6:1-6; 6:14-29). Notice throughout these, that the proclamations of the Lord concerning His sufferings covered three main points:

1. The reference to Himself as "the Son of Man" (8:31; 9:31; 10:45): The Evangelist notes that the "Son of God" became the "The Son of Man," in order to fulfill the will of His Father.

2. The confirmation that He would be killed (8: 31; 9: 31; 10: 34): He came into the world, incarnated, for the purpose of offering Himself as a sacrifice to proclaim His love and save us.

3. The confirmation that He will rise from the dead after three days: Again, His death was not out of weakness, but was done in order to raise us also with Him. With suffering as the foundation of this book, an emphasis on certain parables was made to highlight the suffering that Christ was to endure for our sake. We see this in Christ's explanation of the vineyard and the vinedressers, where the vinedressers planned to kill the heir (12:7). He also spoke of Himself as a cornerstone in which the builders rejected (12:10), and when a woman presented a flask of costly oil to pour it on His head He said, "She has come beforehand to anoint My body for burial" (14:8), etc.

Certain scholars also stress the importance of suffering within the gospel of St. Mark, with one of them in particular commenting that, "This book, as a whole, is a description of how the Lord Jesus has suffered." Another scholar saw in it, "a parade of the sufferings of Christ, either through direct temptations by Satan, or through human sources." This feature led some to believe that St. Mark addressed his book to a particularly suffering Christian community who were facing the burden of persecution, drawing their attention to their duty of sharing the fellowship of suffering with Christ, who invites His disciples to accept it. Some scholars call this book 'the Gospel of the Martyr,' meaning the gospel was presented to support and encourage Christians who face martyrdom.

Whilst the book may not have delved deeply into the philosophy of suffering within the life of Christ, nor that of His disciples, it nevertheless confirmed the commitment to the acceptance of suffering, according to the Will of God.

Christ and His Miracles-
The Fulfilment Of The Law By The Cross

Although most of St. Mark's gospel is focused on Christ who is suffering, a large part of it also rests on presenting Christ as the One who works incessantly for our sake, shown especially through His miracles. The evangelist presents us with 16 stories demonstrating the miracles He performed, confirming that He healed many and cast out several unclean spirits (1:34, 39; 3:10, 11). Interestingly, however, the book also ensures to enunciate the Lord's words, "Why does this generation seek a sign? Assuredly, I say to you, no sign shall be given to this generation." (8:12).

Some, however, distinguish between performing miracles and providing signs from heaven. The Lord performed miracles as acts of love and compassion when He saw His people in need of support, which St. Mark makes sure to note, often writing that Jesus "had compassion on them" and that "He took the children in His arms."

But miracles were not enough for the Pharisees, or King Herod, to accept, as whilst standing before them, they asked for Christ to commit an extraordinary action for the sake of showing or proving Himself. This was something that our Lord utterly refused to do. In this regard, we should notice that:

a) His refusal to give a sign from Heaven was then followed by the admonishing of His disciples to "take heed, beware of the leaven of the Pharisees and the leaven of Herod" (8:15). Upon hearing this, the disciple reasoned among themselves, saying, "It is because we have no bread," even though the Evangelist ensured to mention that "they had one loaf with them in the boat" (8:14). As such, the sign they were asking for was actually right in front of them, but they did not recognise it. We now know its meaning--that the Lord Christ was "the One Loaf" broken for their sake, but they did not know. This was why the Lord rebuked them for not perceiving or understanding (8:17-21). The real unseen sign is the "Eucharistic act," or "the broken loaf that He gave them.

b) Certain scholars believe that the Lord refused to give a sign of Heaven because He wanted them to focus solely on Him. One scholar writes that "Jesus Himself, is the sole sign of the gospel... we should not seek a miracle or sign, separate from Jesus Himself." This idea is based on the saying of the Prophet Isaiah, who wrote that "The Lord Himself will give you a sign: Behold, the virgin shall conceive and bear a Son, and shall call His name Immanuel." (Isaiah 7:14). The sign in which the prophets desired to see, was beholding the incarnate Word of God, our Lord Jesus Christ.

c) Jesus also refused to give them a physical sign, because He came seeking "faith" among the people. The gospel of St. Mark is centred around faith based on trust in Christ Himself and not faith based on signs and visible miracles. The multitude that were astonished (6: 2), quickly commented after Christ's miracles, "Where did this Man get these things? And what wisdom is this, which is given to Him; His hands perform such mighty works! Is not this the carpenter, the Son of Mary...?" (6: 2, 3) Faith, therefore, is not to be based upon the astonishment of a sign or a miracle, but upon leaning on Jesus' bosom, that satisfies the soul.

d) The High Priests and the scribes asked for a sign at the time of crucifixion, saying, "Let the Christ, the King of Israel, descend now from the cross, that we may see and believe" (15:32). They sought a visible sign, namely, descending from the cross, in order to believe in

Him. They did so with the thought that if He had indeed done that, they would have been amazed, the same way we might be by a 'superman.' However, if our Lord had done so, He would not have been able to fulfill His mission as the spiritual King of the Jews. The Lord, in refusing to provide a visible sign by descending from the Cross, was able to attract the heart of the right-hand thief as well as that of the centurion, and to tear the veil of the temple, thus fulfilling the law. The glory of the Cross provided light, not for the purpose of astounding onlookers, but to attract millions to believe in the death and resurrection of the One True Christ. The Cross became a true proclamation and sign that a miracle was performed--not by His descension from the Cross, but through His love and humility, giving Himself up to death and raising again to bring us with Him.

What the High Priests and the scribes did was nothing but an extension of the devil's conversation with the Lord Christ, asking Him to throw Himself down from the pinnacle of the temple to astonish the people to believe in Him. But the way of the Lord Christ is that of the Cross and not by astonishing people with incredible signs!

Indeed, before His crucifixion, He presented to His disciples the sign of His transfiguration on the Mount, right before their eyes. Yet, even then, He did not intend for it to be an astonishing act, but rather working as a gift of divine proclamation. We know this because had this been for an act of amazement, He would not have revealed Himself this way in front of only three of His disciples, but would display it before a great multitude to demonstrate His glory. Our Lord, however, does not do this, and so directs the Transfiguration towards drawing in the disciples' hearts towards a life of fellowship with the Father through His Son and by the Holy Spirit-- through a genuine and intimate experience.

Another way this gospel reveals Christ's desire for faith to be the foundation of our relationship with Him and not just visible miracles, was through its focus on the story of the bleeding woman. When she encountered the Lord, she was blessed by a power that had gone out of

Him (5: 30). It was not through a visible sign or miracle, but through her faith in His ability to heal her that did in fact, heal her.

Finally, whilst the Lord refused to give a sign from Heaven in order to confirm His identity, the antichrists and false prophets conversely express, "show signs and wonders to deceive, if possible, even the elect" (13:21-23).

Jesus the Teacher

The gospel of St. Mark presented our Lord Christ as a Minister to humanity, not just through sermons and commandments, but more so by practical love and Divine compassion, which drew people's souls to Him. The word "teach," (in Greek), is mentioned fifteen times in this book--far more than any of the other books in the New Testament. The Lord Himself, was called "Teacher" seventeen times, not only by Christ Himself (14: 14), but by His disciples, the multitude, and even His adversaries: the Pharisees, the Scribes, the Sadducees, and the Herodians.

The gospel depicts Jesus as a travelling Teacher, moving in every direction and teaching to everyone; whether that be in the synagogue and temple (1:21; 6:2; 11:7; 12:35; 14:49), to the multitude (2:13, 14; 6:34; 10:1) or to His disciples (6:30). In His teachings, Jesus did not follow the typical system of the Rabbis, whereby the disciples would merely be around the Rabbi or attend their preaching. Instead, Christ offered a much more personal relationship with His disciples, encouraging them to accompany their Teacher in true fellowship, living alongside Him intimately.

The main theme of Jesus' teachings extended beyond a list of commandments and precepts, but was more about presenting Himself in a way for them to truly accept Him, although many did not acknowledge Him before His Resurrection. Christ presented Himself as a "sufferer," exhorting His followers to have fellowship with Him throughout His sufferings (8:34; 9:31; 10:32). The reward of this fellowship, Christ taught, was to receive and be joined with Him, having Him in their lives even through the Cross and suffering endured.

Finally, as a Teacher, Christ has been unique in His authority. The Jews and the Gentiles believed in a bitter contest between the Creator and unseen evil, and so the Lord came to cleanse His creation and drive away the unclean spirits used as agents for the evil one. Our Saviour defeated the unseen powers of evil by His death and Resurrection, prevailing over all forms of evil, including those of the Pharisees.

Our Lord in the Gospel of St. Mark

Therefore, the gospel of St. Mark, in its essence, is not a parade of the life of the Lord, but rather a gospel of victory and authority over the powers of evil, presenting Him as a Teacher, Conqueror, and the One who is Victorious!

Whilst this gospel is characterised by its conciseness, it is simultaneously perfectly detailed and clear. There are many examples of St. Mark's attentiveness to detail. It mentions Matthew, the tax collector, as the son of 'Alphaeus' (2:14); the blind Bartimaeus as the son of 'Timaeus' (10:46); Simon, the Cyrenian, as the father of 'Alexander' and 'Rufus' (15:21). Moreover, in his narration of the miracle of feeding the multitude, he was particular in saying that they sat down in groups of hundreds and fifties (6:39, 40). He was also particular in proclaiming the feelings of the Lord Christ, as someone who witnessed His actions, acknowledging Him as a Lover of mankind. He reveals how the Lord partook of our emotions and feelings in empathy, the way someone is when they are very close to us, saying that He was "moved with compassion" (1:41). "looked at the young man and loved him" (10:21), "took the children in His arms" (9:36; 1:16) and many other instances alike.

St. Mark was also fond of using the expression, "immediately," in order to offer the reader the same feeling that he himself had of Christ's action-based love. This again, relates to what the Romans valued as he was writing to them. The gospel uses present tense to narrate certain incidents, creating a continuous stream of actions that Christ did during His ministry.

Interestingly, the evangelist was the one one to mention the miracles of healing the deaf and the mute (7:31-37), as well as the healing of the blind paralytic of Bethsaida (8:22-27); and the parable of scattered seed (4:26-29).

The gospel of
ST LUKE

INTRODUCTION

The word "Luke" is probably an abbreviation of the Latin word "Lucanus" or "Lucius," which means 'the carrier of the light' or 'the enlightened.' However, we are yet to differentiate between the evangelist St. Luke, and Lucuis, who was mentioned in Acts 31: 1 as well as in Rom 6: 21.

He is the only one among the writers of the New Testament who was not a Jew, but a Gentile, and was likely from Antioch in Syria. St. Luke accepted the Christian faith unhesitatingly, without becoming a Jew. We know this through the scribes, who note this when saying that St. Paul the apostle, who mentioned St. Luke in the epistle to the Colossians (4: 14), did not include St. Luke among those who were circumcised (4: 10, 11), along with Aristreches and Mark, Barabes' nephew, and Jesus called Justus.

ABOUT THE AUTHOR

Some think that he is one of the seventy apostles, as well as one of the two disciples, to whom Jesus appeared to after His resurrection on their way to Amos (Luke 24: 12), but that the apostle did not mention his name due to the spirit of humility. The majority of people within these modern studies, however, do not believe that he was one of the apostles, but that he rather accepted the faith at the hands of St. Paul the apostle. They pointed this out primarily due to the fact that there was a lack of historical evidence supporting this, alongside the fact that this idea seems to contradict the gospel introduction, as the writer says about the matters concerning the Lord Jesus (Luke 1: 2), "Even as they delivered them unto us, which from the beginning were eyewitnesses and ministers of the word." It is as if the writer had not seen the Lord Jesus, but has rather recorded what has been handed over through copying the records in great accuracy, confirming it by those who have witnessed it themselves. Maybe it was for this reason, that a scholar of the comments on the gospel has said, "It is the outcome of the collective faith, based on the copying of, and not an individual work."

St. Luke was also a physician (Col 4: 14) and a painter. It is noted in the tradition of copying, that he has painted the icon of the Virgin St. Mary. St. Luke was also attached to St. Paul, the apostle for the Gentiles. In the Acts of the Apostles, they set out together from the forum Troas to Samothracia, and the next day to Neapolis, and from there, to Philippi (Acts 16: 10-39, the second preaching trip). At another time during the journey of St. Paul the apostle, St. Luke also followed him on the way back from Philippi to Jerusalem (Acts 20: 5; 21: 18). Moreover, he escorted St. Paul in Rome while imprisoned (Acts 28: 30), and in his last moments, St. Luke was with St. Paul, for the latter says in his farewell epistle (2 Tim 4: 11) "Only Luke is with me."

In this way, they were both bonded together. The evangelist St. Luke recorded for us a great deal about God's preaching and work through St. Paul the apostle in the Acts of the Apostles. He was called by St. Paul (Col 4: 14), "Luke, the beloved physician," and in Philippians he called St. Luke 'the one who worked with him.'

It is said he lived a virgin and that he worked in Achacia in Greece. He was martyred at the age of eighty-four, and that the emperor, Constantinos II, transferred his remains to Constantinople in the year 357 AD. In the year 1177 AD, they were transferred to Padua in Italy.

THE GOSPEL'S AUDIENCE

God the Heavenly Friend

Our teacher, St. Matthew the herald, being a Jew, wrote to the Jews to declare that Jesus is the Messiah and King. It was He who's coming was long awaited by the fathers and prophets, so they have a share in the eternal spiritual kingdom. St. Mark wrote to the Romans, to declare Christ as the servant working, not through the spirit of temporary authority, loftiness, and violence, but rather through the spirit of sacrifice. He would save by means of his deeds of love, and not by means of armies and temporary powers. As for our teacher St. Luke the herald, an educated Gentile and physician, he wished to serve those of the Hellenistic concepts, and thus wrote to the Greeks about the Lord Jesus as being 'a friend to the entirety of humanity!' He presented His divine deeds for salvation to fulfill what the Greek philosophy and human wisdom were unable to fulfill. This is why this gospel is called 'the gospel of God's friendship' or 'the gospel of Jesus the Saviour.' It was furthermore called 'the universal gospel,' since it represents an invitation to all of humanity to accept the call of the Heavenly Friend and react with His deed of salvation through love.

The aim of 'God the Friend' is seen most clearly in our discussion of the traits of this book. St. Luke wrote this gospel to his dear friend, Theophilus (Luke 1: 3), to which its title, 'dear', is an honourable one. This is why the majority of people think he is of honourable peers, of an Antiochan origin, such as St. Luke the herald himself, and so wrote to him as a Gentile, like himself. He is not alone to benefit from it, but as the scholar Oregandes says, for the triumphant ones of the Gentiles in general to benefit from it as well. Some have thought that this Luke was a slave to his master, the Gentile Theophilus, and since he, as a physician, cured him, he rewarded him by being released from bondage. Hence, the physician Luke sent him this gospel as a sign of his gratitude and appreciation. Others said the word 'Theophilus', which means 'God's lover', is only a covered name for one of the dignitaries in Alexandria. But the evangelist did not reveal this, so that he would not be subjected to hardships due to his Christianity. At any rate, this book is addressed to the Gentiles in general to be blessed with the heavenly Friend, as a saviour for the soul.

Time and Place of Writing

There is no sure information concerning the time of this gospel's writing, or its site. St. Irianus believes it was written before the martyrdom of St. Paul, whereas St. Jerome believes it was written afterwards, based on the historian Yousspios El Kaisarry's words. Since the gospel was written prior to the book of Acts, and the book of Acts was written before the martyrdom of St. Paul the apostle (with no mention made of the event), many students believe it was written between the years 63 and 67 AD. It was likely written in Rome, although some others believe it was written in Achacia, or in Alexandria.

The church records in the first century that the writer of this gospel and the book of the Acts of the Apostles is St. Luke the herald, and that he was the apostle's escort. This is also made clear by the writings of the forefathers: Justin the martyr, Irianus, Oreganus, and Tertullian, to which the same evidence exists.

In addition to these bits of evidence, the book itself carries information that its writer is our teacher, St. Luke. Among these is the fact that the book is addressed to Theophilus, the one and same person to whom Acts of the Apostles was addressed to. In addition to this is the introduction of the Acts of the Apostles, which actually completes the ending of St. Luke's gospel, since the writer is one and the same. The two books are similar in linguistics, style of writing, and thought. Furthermore, the accurate expressions he used in describing the diseases the Lord Jesus cured, point to the fact that the writer was a physician. As a physician who held respect to the medical profession, he did not describe what St. Mark the apostle mentioned about the woman who was persistently bleeding in the same way, (Mark 5: 26) "And had suffered many things of many physicians, and had spent all that she had, and was nothing bettered, but rather grew worse." He instead, thought it was enough to say (Luke 8: 43) "And a woman having an issue of blood twelve years, which had spent all her living upon physicians, neither could be healed of any."

HOW THE GOSPEL IS ARRANGED

The Structure of the Gospel and the Old Testament

Some scholars believe that St. Luke's gospel follows the pattern of the first six books of the Old Testament, in the following way:

1. The new book (new book meaning the stages of Jesus' life analogous to the Old Testament books) of Genesis describes the birth of the Lord Jesus and his childhood by means of which the new creation is fulfilled. With the appearance of the second Adam, humanity has been released into the new world

2. The new Exodus has been fulfilled by the tribulation of the Lord Jesus in the wilderness for forty days, where He overcame temptation. This is an opposite situation to the maze that the people of Israel faced for forty years after their departure, and their perpetual fall into complaints and grumbling.

3. The book of the new Leviticus is the establishing of the twelve disciples, and presenting the sermon, which concerns their ordainment (St. Luke 6:20 etc.).

4. The book of the new Numbers is the mission of the seventy apostles.

5. The special part in the book of Deuteronomy represents a major part of the gospel, since it comprises many sections of the Lord's teachings, particularly in Luke 9: 51, 18: 14.

6. The book of Joshua that was presented by our teacher St. Luke is the story of the Lord's suffering and His resurrection. Through the acceptance of Rahab, the prostitute is faced by Zacchaeus the tax collector (Luke 19: 1, 2).

The gospel of St. Luke can be divided into five major sections:

1. Our Friend who became like us, Chapters 1-3

2. Our Friend who is tempted like us, Chapter 4

3. Our Friend who feels our suffering, Chapters 5-18

4. Our faithful Friend, Chapters 19-23

5. Our Friend, the Risen from the dead, Chapter 24

MAIN THEMES IN THE GOSPEL OF ST. LUKE

Special Features of the Gospel of St. Luke

Because the evangelist presented the Lord Jesus as being 'the Saviour, the Friend to humanity', it is why he spoke so many times of 'the Son of Man', who came to us and embodied our humanity so as to grant us the partnership of his divine nature. Greek philosophy had merely offered concepts, which is something that cannot dwell in the heart and change its depths. But as for the Son of Man, He came as a friend to man, to be accepted inwardly, and by means of this unique friendship, he would be granted tremendous abilities working in his depths which are reflected in his behaviour. By calling the Lord 'the Son of Man', it brings down and removes our feelings of estrangement to God, or His estrangement to us, for He has come down to us, to escort us on our way.

Christ as the Friend to All

The most important quality of this gospel may be that it presents 'the Savior, the Friend' to all of humanity, for it is a gospel to the universe. It is a call to everyone, and not only to the Jews. This is why we notice the following:

1. Due to the fact that the Jews looked upon themselves as righteous people, and all the other nations as sinners, the evangelist declares the

Lord Jesus as 'the Friend to sinners.' He was the only one to say the Son of Man has come (Luke 19: 10) "to seek and to save that, which was lost." Moreover, he has presented to us a significant number of the Lord's sayings and His parables, showing the friendship of the Lord Jesus and His companionship with sinners, such as the particular parable of longsuffering on the old barren fig-tree (Luke 13: 6-9). Also, the parable of the lost sheep, the missing coin, and the prodigal son (Luke15). He also told us of the sinful woman (Luke 7: 36-50), and the repentance of Zacchaeus the tax collector (Luke 19: 1-10), as well as the promise to the repentant thief on the cross (Luke 23: 40-43), etc.

2. He quoted expressions and events that opened the doors of hope to the Gentiles, such as Isaiah the prophet who said, "every being will see the Lord's salvation." Also, Elijah the prophet's message to Sarepta, a city of Sidon, unto a woman that was a widow (Luke 4: 25), and (Luke 4: 27), which mentions, "And many lepers were in Israel in the time of Eliseus the prophet; and none of them was cleansed, saving Naaman the Syrian."

3. He mentioned the dispatch of the seventy apostles. If the twelve disciples represent the call to the Jews (the twelve tribes), then the number 70 points to the fullness of the Gentiles.

4. In the genealogy of the Lord Jesus, he did not begin with Abraham, but rather with Adam, the father of all mankind (Luke 3: 28).

The progressive Gospel - A focus on Women and Children

Because it is the book of the divine friendship towards man, 'man', in this instance, also refers to the friendship that is also offered to the children and women. He sanctified childhood and uplifted the position of women, and their positive role. He also paid special concern to the poor, the needy, and those exiled and in bondage.

Concerning children, St. Luke was also the only one to mention the birth of John the Baptist and his childhood. Moreover, he was the only one to mention in detail the annunciation of the Virgin with the birth of the Baby Jesus, and the embryo's joy in Elizabeth's womb when Saint Mary came in to greet her. St. Luke was also the one to mention the circumcision of the Baby Jesus, going into the temple with St. Mary on the fortieth day, and His going to the temple He was only twelve years of age, etc. All four of these events were mentioned in detail.

With regards to women, some scholars noticed that St. Luke the evangelist, since he presented the catholic universal gospel, had given special attention to women, more so than the other evangelists. In the Hellenic world, it seemed as though a woman's social status according to the law, were more progressive than that of the Jews at that time. This is why the evangelist wished to prove the gospel message was unrestricted by the Jewish tradition. The evangelist was the only one to also mention the widow, Hennah, who worshiped in the temple (Luke 2: 36). He also recorded to us Martha's service and her sister Mary's sitting at the Saviour's feet, listening to His words.

Special Care for the Poor, the Sick, and the Needy

The evangelist was concerned about the poor, the needy and those in exile. He reveals this in his special attention to the good news being delivered to St. Mary, a poor girl in Nazareth, as well as detailing the story of the angel with the simple and modest shepherds. The Lord also spoke of the rich man and the poor, as well as the sick. St. Luke also detailed the parable of the Good Samaritan, the parable of the tax-collector, the story of the prostitute in the house of Simon the Pharisee, the parable of the prodigal son, the story of Mary Magdalene, and the acceptance of the repentant thief on the cross, etc. One scholar wrote that "he showed concern about the minorities, and the forgotten, rejected people such as the Samaritans, the lepers, the tax-collectors, the soldiers, and the sinners in general who are in humiliation. He also mentioned the Gentile shepherds and the poor – all of whom find encouragement in this gospel."

Some, such as Leon-Dufour, think that the expression 'the social gospel' could be said about the gospel of our teacher St. Luke the evangelist.

This is due to the fact that he has mentioned a great deal about the obligation of giving to the poor (Luke 3: 10; 14: 12-14). He declared the penalty for those who do not share in supplying their needs (Luke 16: 25) and also made it a clear point to not inflict injustice or betrayal onto anyone.

It is difficult to speak of a gospel as a social one or a spiritual one, because the life of faith is a unified entity, an inseparable one. If the spiritual work is presented, then the social aspect is not to be disregarded. Also, as in the opposite case, if the social work is presented, it is of a spiritual actuality. What the evangelist ensured to point out, however, regarding the poor, the needy, those suffering, and those who have been wronged, is that all of these are normal outcomes once tasting the Lord Jesus' friendship. Whilst we might suffer for following Chris, it is in these instances where our Lord reveals Himself as the Friend concerned about us all, particularly those in spiritual need, materialistic need, social or physiological need. It is appropriate for us, being His friends, to repay His love with our own and to carry His qualities in us. For what He offers us, obliges us to offer in return in some way or another to our brethren.

The Gospel of Daily, Unconditional Love and Mercy

As a Friend of ours, Christ does not only offer us salvation on the cross, but He also offers us a love that enters our daily life. We see Him sharing supper at the house of Simon the Pharisee, accepting the banquet of Zacchaeus the tax-collector, and responding to the invitation of Amos' disciples and their welcome to Him. As a Friend, He does not ask for violence or for fanaticism. We therefore see him rebuking John for asking that fire descend to consume the Samaritan people (Luke 9: 54). He moreover rebuked the disciples saying, "he that is not against us is for us" (Luke 9: 50). It is the 'gospel of mercy' or 'the gospel of great forgiveness.' As a Friend of ours, He is eager for us to accept His friendship and respond to His love. This is why he often urges us to accept his friendship by drawing comparisons between different people, such as:

1. Simon the Pharisee and the sinful woman: Simon had offered his house and a banquet, but not whole-heartedly; whereas the woman, despite her sins but because of her love, was able to receive the blessings of Christ's friendship and forgiveness.

2. The Pharisee and the tax-collector: the Pharisee went into the temple, having Mosaic deeds that he cherishes, yet in his pride he was unable to befriend the Lord; whereas the tax-collector was able to, though in the last row, enter the heart of the greatest Friend by means of his modesty and humility.

3. The Good Samaritan, the Levite and the priest: the former was able to enter the Lord's friendship by means of his open-hearted love to mankind; whereas the servers of religion, lost their friendship through their unloving and hardened hearts.

4. The prodigal son and the older brother: the prodigal son obtained the blessing and enjoyed the friendship by means of his repentance and his return; whereas the elder son lost his relationship with the father due to his pride.

5. The repentant thief and the thief that perished: the former entered the kingdom of heaven in his last moments.

6. The Beatitudes and the Woes.

Christ as the only One to offer True Joy

Although Greek thinking prevailed over the world at that time, it did not offer humanity true joy. Men lived asking each day for a new philosophy or concept unheard of before. This is why the evangelist wrote this book to announce that Christ is the Friend to all mankind, and that it is He who grants inward joy and peace. The book includes a significant number of praising hymns that the church cherishes and uses during its worship and liturgies, such as the angelic hymn of the birth (Luke 2:

14), as well as Zacharias' hymns of praise (Luke 1: 46-55), and the hymn of the elderly Simon (Luke 2: 29-32).

The coming of the Friend and the Saviour, created an atmosphere of joy. The book opens with the angels' words to Zacharias about the forerunner to our Saviour and Friend, saying, "And thou shalt have joy and gladness; and many shall rejoice at his birth" (Luke 1:14). He also narrates how His birth overjoyed so many people (Luke 1: 58). But as for the Lord's Birth, this was accomplished by the opening of heaven on earth, as it was proclaimed, "for, behold, I bring you good tidings of great joy, which shall be to all people" (Luke 2: 10). When the seventy apostles returned after their preaching, "And the seventy returned again with joy, saying, Lord, even the devils are subject unto us through thy name," (Luke 10: 17) it was then said, "In that hour Jesus rejoiced in spirit, and said, I thank thee, O Father, Lord of heaven and earth, that thou hast hid these things from the wise and prudent, and hast revealed them unto babes: even so, Father; for so it seemed good in thy sight" (Luke 10: 21).

It was as if the preaching of the unequaled Friend had brought joy to the Saviour's heart Himself for the sake of the meek, which is of pleasure to the Father. He even declared that there would be joy in the heavens at the repentance of one sinner (Luke 15: 7, 10, 32). It is an inward joy that fills the heart of the repentant sinner when he finds satisfaction in his friend, for it was said of Zacchaeus, "And he made haste, and came down, and received him joyfully" (Luke 19: 6). He was also joyful for all people, as it was said, "and all the people rejoiced for all the great works He did" (Luke 13: 7). This was also seen in His entering into Jerusalem, "the whole multitude of the disciples began to rejoice and praise God with a loud voice for all the mighty works that they had seen" (Luke 19: 37).

The book concludes with the joy of the Friend being raised from the dead and ascending to the heavens. It is said that the disciples, upon the reappearance of their amazing Friend, that they "...yet believed not for joy, and wondered..." (Luke 24: 41). Also, after His ascension, the disciples, "...worshipped him, and returned to Jerusalem with great joy" (Luke 24: 57).

In this way, the Lord Jesus came to fulfill the Father's pleasure, rejoicing at humanity being saved by His blood, with the heavens rejoicing with Him. This is, in the same way, Christ filling His apostles and disciples with joy, pouring it onto the Church with His gladness, as well on the repentant sinners.

To differentiate between this joy and the temporary joy of the world, He gives us the parable of the foolish rich man who said to himself, "Soul, thou hast much goods laid up for many years; take thine ease, eat, drink, and be merry" (Luke 12: 19). But he could not rejoice, for he heard the godly voice saying, "Thou fool, this night thy soul shall be required of thee" (Luke 12: 20). All of this is what made some call the gospel of St. Luke, 'the gospel of the Mosaic joy.'

Christ as an example and Role Model

Because the Lord Jesus came as a friend to us, He gave us Himself as an example. He appeared praying on many occasions, as on His baptism (Luke 3: 21), after cleansing the leper, before calling the twelve disciples (Luke 6: 12), and also at the transfiguration (Luke 9: 28). Moreover, He prayed on the cross for those who crucified Him during His last moments of His life on earth. He wished to declare that 'prayer' is a mystery that develops our relationship or friendship with God. The Lord, when praying, also reveals that He carries us in Him, and through Him we are connected to the Father. The Lord speaks to us of prayer in the gospel of St. Luke more than in the other gospels. In it is mentioned the Lord's Prayer, as well as Christ stressing the importance of constant and persistent prayer. He gave us the parable of the person who was in need of three loaves of bread, and how he went to his friend asking in persistence to show this. He also gave us the parable of the unjust judge who heard the widow's pleadings and answered her.

Christ and the Church

Some believe that across all of the gospels, and in St. Luke's gospel in particular, they did not aim for merely speaking about the life of the

Lord Jesus or His history, but rather that it was aimed at presenting the Church in which the Lord lived for. It actually speaks of Christ's church, that she (the church) tasted Him, by encompassing Him and being firm in Him. St. Luke in his gospel also reveals the inspiration of the Holy Spirit and the Church life whilst Christ was physically present on earth. By contrast, in the book of Acts, St. Luke presents the life of the Church with her Groom whilst He was seated at the right hand of the Father after His ascension, and how he granted the Church his Holy Spirit. He is the active Friend, working unceasingly. He worked when He was here in the body, and He is still working after His ascension until He meets the Church in the Heavens.

In the first church there prevailed the feeling that the coming of the Lord Jesus drew very near, and that it would be fulfilled in the apostolic age. This issue was tackled by St. Paul the apostle in his second epistle to the people of Thessalonica. He confirmed that the Lord would not be manifested until after the appearance of the man of sin, and the rebounding act is fulfilled. Our teacher, St. Luke, followed the same path, declaring in his book, as well as in the book of Acts, that the Lord's death, His resurrection, and His glorious ascension, do not mean that His second coming would be instant. Neither will it be right after the desolation of Jerusalem; for some have misunderstood the words of St. Mark the evangelist (Mark 14: 62; 9: 1) in that regard. St. Mark declared that the Messiah's kingdom is fulfilled here at the church first; and that it is fulfilled in the heart. Every day there are those who are saved, who come to join the church. It is as if the Lord's coming is fulfilled first by His dwelling in the hearts of the many, and when His work is completed here on earth, He returns by the clouds.

The Holy Spirit and Jesus' Parables

The evangelist St. Luke clearly showed the role of the Holy Spirit. He does so when the angel declared that John the Baptist was full of the Holy Spirit from his mother's womb (Luke 1: 15), as well as through revealing the work of the Holy Spirit in the divine incarnation (Luke 1: 35), and his work in the words of prophecy (Luke 1: 67; 2: 25-27). He also shows it in the baptism (Luke 3: 22). In this way, the work of the Lord Jesus is linked to the work of His Holy Spirit (Luke 4: 1, 14, 18; 10: 21; 11: 13, 10, 12).

This book has been called the gospel of coverage; it contains a great number of stories that were not mentioned in the other gospels, alongside many other parables. He was able to do this due to his good relationship with St. Mary.

He is different to the other gospels by mentioning the following miracles: the catching of the fish (Luke 5: 4-11), raising the widow's son of Nain (Luke 7: 11), the woman who had an infirm spirit (Luke 13: 11-17), the leprous man (Luke 14: 1-6), the ten lepers (Luke 17: 11-19), and the healing of Malachi's ear (Luke 22: 50, 51).

He is also singled out in mentioning the following parables: the two debtors (Luke 7: 41- 43), the Good Samaritan (Luke 14: 25-37), the persistent friend (Luke 11: 5-8), the foolish rich man (Luke 12: 12-16), the barren fig tree (Luke 13: 6-9), the lost piece of silver (Luke 15: 8-10), the prodigal son (Luke 15: 11-30), the unfaithful steward (Luke 16: 1-13), the rich man and Lazarus (Luke 16: 19-31), the Pharisee and the tax collector (Luke 18: 10-14). He was also the only one to mention certain incidents, such as John the Baptist's role to the people, Jews crying overview Jerusalem, the topic of his speech with Moses and Elijah at the transfiguration, the sweat that dropped forum His forehead like drops of blood, His talking to the daughters of Jerusalem, the Lord's encounter with the Amos disciples, and also certain details that concern His ascension.

The Unique Linguistics of the Gospel

From a linguistic perspective, we have said before on more than one occasion that the Holy Spirit works in the writer and inspires him in his writing, yet He does not make him lose his identity. Rather, He makes use of the writer's abilities, inspires him and protects him from making any errors. The perspective of our teacher St. Luke the evangelist, was manifested through his particular style. As a physician, he investigated meticulously into many of the issues. Moreover, as a physician and a painter at the same time, he was gentle in his writing style, with touches of sweet poetry, to the extent that his gospel became a source for artists to be inspired when painting icons. Because he was a friend and escort of St. Paul on many of his journeys, there developed some similarities between their writings, which made the scholar Tritilian say that St. Luke the evangelist was enlightened by St. Paul the apostle. (See Luke 4: 22, with Col 4: 6; like 4: 32 with 1Cor 2: 4; Luke 6: 36 with 2Cor 1: 3; Luke 6: 39 with Rom 2: 19; Luke 9: 56 with 2Cor 10: 18; Luke 10: 8 with 1Cor 10: 23; Luke 11: 41 with Titus 1: 15; Luke 18: 1 with 2Thes 1: 11; Luke 21: 36 with Eph 6: 18; Luke 22: 19, 20 with 1Cor 23-29; Luke 24: 34 with 1Cor 15: 5).

The gospel of
ST JOHN

INTRODUCTION

The Gospel according to St. John answers the needs of everyone: both the simple person and the scholar. In saying this, St. John's words are mostly simple, and so people who are simple in their faith find themselves closely drawn and comforted by St. John's gospel. On the other hand, those with spiritual experience find the opportunity to dive into his writings without ever fully reaching the true depth of this gospel.

The Gospel of St. John
and the Early Church

The Gospel according to St. John attracted the heart of the early Church and lifted it to perceive the sublime, divine mysteries. This is the result of the inspiration of the Holy Spirit. Moreover, St. John uses a style that is spiritually attractive, and which is far removed from difficult philosophical terms or dry theological language. Below are excerpts from some of our Church Fathers on the Gospel according to St. John:

We may understand the Gospels to be the first-born of all the Holy Books, and that from among the Gospels, the first-born of them all, is the Gospel of St. John. Unless we lean on the Lord's bosom (Jn 13:23) and accept St. Mary through Jesus Christ as our Mother (Jn 19:27), we will not understand its message. By doing so, we become another St.

John ourselves, and the Lord Jesus Christ will appear to us just as He had appeared to St. John. According to those who have presented a truthful report about St. Mary, she had no son other than the Lord Jesus Christ. Jesus had said to His Mother about St. John, "This is your son" (Jn 19:26). He did not say: "This is your son as well." It is as though He was telling her: "This is Jesus whom you have conceived." Indeed, every person who has become perfect does not live but rather it is Christ who lives in him (2 Cor 4:7). And since Christ lives in him, it is possible to refer to him and tell St. Mary: "Here is your son, Jesus Christ."

Origen

All the others - the evangelists Mathew, Mark, and Luke - have risen slightly above earthly matters. That is, they have dealt with the events that Jesus did on earth, while they spoke only briefly about His divinity. They seemed to be just like other people who had accompanied Him on earth. By contrast, the Eagle - that is St. John - was the one to preach the sublime Truth, as well as the one who contemplates and turns with piercing vision towards the inner eternal Light... In spite of that, we are the ones who are weak and crawl upon the earth: we walk among men with difficulty, we venture to uphold and comprehend these sublime matters, and we lead ourselves to believe that we have comprehended these issues since we have meditated on them or spoken about them.

St. Augustine

As for the blessed St. John...we find that he possesses a fiery desire and a mind that yearns for matters which surpass the human mind. He ventures and draws close in order to explain the sublime Birth which is impossible to report in its totality – the Birth of God, the Word. Yet he realises that, "it is the glory of God to conceal matters" (Prov 25:2); and that the honour due to God exceeds our understanding and comprehension. Hence, it is hard for anyone to understand or explain the features of the Divine nature.

St. Cyril, the Great

ABOUT THE AUTHOR

The word John means "Jehovah is tender." He is the son of Zebedee from the house of Sidon in Galilee, and the Lord Jesus Christ called him and his older brother James, to follow him. Herod Agrippas, the First, killed James in the year 44 BC.

It seems that St. John was relatively well off, as his father used to hire men to handle his boats (Mk 1:20). Moreover, the high priest knew who John was (Jn 8:16). His mother, Salome, was a virtuous and pious woman who always followed the Lord (Mk 15:40). She participated with the other women in buying expensive spices for the body of Jesus. It is most likely the case that she is the sister of Mary, the mother of the Lord Jesus Christ (Jn 19:25).

St. John as a disciple of Christ

He became a fisherman by trade, and he and his brother James were fishing partners with Simon and Andrew (Lk 5:10). The Lord Jesus Christ chose Simon, Andrew, John, and James to be His first disciples. Because John and his brother had very fiery tempers the Lord named them 'Boanerges', which means the 'sons of thunder' (Mk 3:17). John, however, became known as the apostle of love. He was extremely gentle, and his gospel, letters and revelations all revolve around 'love.' He continued to preach about love until his old age. In his interpretation of the Epistle of St. Paul the Apostle to the Galatians, St. Jerome reports that in his old age, the disciples of John used to carry him and take him up into the pulpit to hear him utter these words, "My children love one another. This is the Lord's commandment: if you follow just this one commandment, it will be good enough for you." John is known as the 'disciple whom Jesus loved' (Jn 21:20).

St. Irenaeus reports that John was twenty-five years old when the Lord Jesus called him to be His disciple. Like Peter and James, John is considered to be one of the special ones, who were privileged enough to be alone with the Lord Jesus in many instances, such as at the Transfiguration (Matt 17:1), raising of the daughter of Jarius (Mk

5:37), in the Garden of Gethsemane (Matt 26:37) and the time the Lord predicted the destruction of the Temple in Jerusalem (Mk 13:3). The Lord entrusted him and Peter to prepare the place where He would hold the Passover with the disciples (Lk 22:8).

St. John in particular, leant on the Lord's chest (Lk 13:23) and he accompanied the Lord and stood at the foot of the Cross where he received St. Mary as his mother (Jn 19:20-27).

St. John's work after the Resurrection of Jesus Christ

After the resurrection of the Lord, he was with Peter when he healed the lame man at the gate of the temple that is called Beautiful (Acts 3:1-6). He was also with Peter when they were sent to Samaria to lay their hands on believers so that they might receive the Holy Spirit (Acts 8:14-17). St. Paul considered him to be one of the pillars of the Church (Acts 15:6; Gal 22:9).

He preached in the Asia Minor, namely in Ephesus; was tortured under Dematious and was exiled to the Island of Patmos. It was there where he enjoyed the revelations concerning the Day of the Lord: The book of Revelations of Jesus Christ. He remained in exile until his death.

According to St. Jerome, St. John remained in the world for sixty-eight years after the resurrection of the Lord Jesus Christ. Based on that, he lived for two or more years into the second century A.D. This means that he lived to be almost one hundred, for he was a few years younger than the Lord. Others believe that he died in the year 98 A.D. during the reign of Trojan (98-117 A.D.).

In his book 'The History of the Church,' Eusebius the Caesarian recounts a story about St. John the apostle. It reveals how much he was concerned, even in his old age, about the salvation of the human soul and the amazing ways he used to fulfill that task. The historian borrowed the story from the book written by St. Clement of Alexandria, titled, 'Who is the Rich Person Who will be Redeemed?" The story recounts that after St. John returned from the Island of Patmos, he went to the city of Ephesus to resolve ecclesiastical matters and to appoint bishops.

Stories of St. John bringing people to the Church

He also visited some of the neighbouring pagan areas. In one of these cities close by, probably Izmir, he introduced to the bishop of the local church a young pagan who had accepted the faith. St. John was very concerned about him and underlined that the youth would be a trust that he would deliver into the bishop's hands. The latter consequently tended him until he was baptised. However, the youth soon made the acquaintance of some corrupt youngsters who encouraged him to lead a life of pleasure and squandering. When they needed money, they resorted to stealing and he would join them. Thus, he became progressively involved in one crime after another, and he even formed and led a gang to steal, plunder and kill. Eventually, St. John returned to the city and asked the bishop about the youth. The bishop informed him, "He was led astray…he spiritually died, for he has reverted to his evil days and has become an indecent person and a robber. Instead of being a Church member, he has gone to the mountains with a gang who shared his disposition." The saint could not bear the news and asked for a horse that he mounted in spite of his old age. He rode to the area where the robbers hid, and they captured him and carried him to their leader. Upon seeing the saint, the gangster felt so embarrassed that he tried to flee. However, St. John ran after him and shouted, "Why are you running away from me? My son, I am your father and I am harmless and advanced in age. If need be, I am willing to die for your sake just as the Lord Jesus Christ suffered death on our behalf. For your sake, I will sacrifice my life. Stop. Believe, for the Lord has sent me to you." The youth instantly felt ashamed and stopped. He held his head down and spread his arms in fear while he wept bitterly. St. John was overjoyed and led him back to Church, where he stayed with him until he felt assured he would be well.

St. John Cassian also tells the following story:

"As St. John was one day coddling an eagle, a young hunter came by and wondered at the sight. He asked the saint why a great man like him would waste his time as such. The saint responded by asking him: "What are you holding in your hand?" The youth answered: "It is a bow." The saint said, "And why is it loose?" The youth replied: "Because if it remains taut all the time it loses its flexibility which is what I need to have when I shoot an arrow." The old saint said, "Therefore you should not be upset with me, my young friend, because I sometimes release the strings of my soul. Otherwise I would lose its power and I would be let down when I turn to it in the time I need.""

St. John's Strength in maintaining the Truth of Christ

The historian, Eusebius, also reports how St. John was extremely concerned about preserving the upright faith from the trends of heretic thoughts. He bases his report on the writings of St. Clement, bishop of Lyon. He reports that the Saint went into a public bath to bathe, and there he heard the heretic Kirnasius (proclaiming that the kingdom of the Lord Jesus Christ is an earthly one; and that He loved to go to dinners and engage in impure physical relationships). Upon hearing that, St. John jumped out in great dismay, and ran away as he could not bear to be under the same roof with that man. He told his companions to follow his example and said, "Let us escape lest the bath would collapse due to the presence of Kirnasius, who is the enemy of truth".

Using the words of Apollonius, who is believed to have been a bishop of Ephesus, Eusebius the historian, also tells us that the apostle St. John, by the grace of God, raised a person from the dead.

The Scholar Tertullian reports that St. John was thrown into a tub filled with boiling oil and that the Lord rescued him.

THE GOSPEL'S AUDIENCE

The Aim of the Gospel of St. John, Jesus as the Messiah

The Evangelist tells us about his objective in writing the gospel through the following words, "…that you may believe that Jesus is the Christ, the Son of God, and that believing you may have life in His name" (Jn 20:31). Note that the word 'believe', in this verse, occurs in Greek as 'pioteonte', which also appears in the Seniaid, Vatican, and Koredethi versions. It is used in the present tense and not in the past tense, indicating that the Gospel has been written to reinforce a faith that is established already. Hence, he is not presenting a new faith, but rather he seeks to uphold the faith of the church, which she (the church) already enjoys, seeking to prevent anyone from deflecting from it.

The core of our faith is that Jesus is the Messiah and the Son of God. According to W.C. Van Unnick, the word 'Messiah' is not a mere title, but it actually means 'the One anointed', or, 'The anointed King.' Whilst this was not an issue for the Gentiles, it is the main problem for the Jews to recognise or accept. As for the expression 'Son of God', the Hellenic world was able to understand and recognise it more than others. In any case, the association of the two expressions was fundamental to indoctrinate and ascertain the faith of those from Jewish or Gentile origins. Every believer must recognise that Jesus is the subject of all the old prophecies, and that He is the Son of God and is consubstantial with Him in essence. Hence, He is able to offer redemption and renew our nature. Scholars have remarked that the word 'Messiah' occurs in this gospel only without any translation and just in its own right. It is as though St. John intends to underline the concept of the Jews. Consequently, we find him presenting us with the words of Philip to Nathaniel, "We have found Him of whom Moses in the law, and also the prophets, wrote…" (Jn 1:45).

This is also revealed when Andrew says to his brother Simon Peter, "We have found the Messiah" (which is translated, the Christ) (Jn 1:41). This is the picture of the Lord Jesus Christ that we find in the Gospel of

St. John from its very beginning--a Messianic picture. It is the picture of Christ as the King and Messiah that the Jews have awaited for so long, and Whom the Evangelist certifies in more than one passage. He reports that when the Lord entered Jerusalem, they, "...cried out: 'Hosanna! Blessed is He who comes in the name of the Lord! The King of Israel!'...His disciples did not understand these things at first; but when Jesus was glorified, then they remembered that these things were written about Him" (Jn 12:13-16). Before Pilate, the Lord admitted that He had a Kingdom (Jn 18:33-37). He was claimed as King of the Jews (Jn 19:3, 12-15, 19, 20).

St. John is the only one who reports that the crowds sought Him to crown Him as King, but he withdrew from their midst (6:15). The Lord did so because their concept of a Messianic King was different from His own. This presentation of the Lord Jesus Christ as the Messiah King whom the Jews had been waiting for so long, led some scholars to consider that St. John was a Jewish man with a bitter heart. They explain that this was due to the enmity that the Jews expressed towards the Lord Jesus Christ. This is what Lord Charnwood claimed in 1925. However, some scholars, such as F.Taylor, observed that this was not the main objective, and that St. John was bitter towards anyone who expressed hostility towards the Lord, whether that came from a Jew or from a non-Jew. Other scholars, such as A.T. Robinson, found that the Apostle did not direct his gospel to the Jews, but rather to Christians of Hellenic origin.

The aim of this Gospel is to ascertain the Divinity of the Lord Jesus Christ, as He is the Son of God. The Apostle had no intention of going into theoretical discussions or philosophical arguments. He just proposed that we enjoy life in His Name. Our faith in the Lord's divinity touches our lives and redeems our very souls. Consequently, after the New Testament had been written, the first sermon we find in our hands begins with these words, "It is appropriate for us, dear brethren, to think of the Lord Jesus Christ as the Son of God, the Judge of the living and the dead. Therefore, we should not belittle the issue of our redemption, for if we do, we will be belittling (the Lord Jesus Christ) and will consequently receive so little from Him." It is as though this gospel comes to claim, with greater clarity and elaboration, what the other evangelists have presented to us. It announces the divine aspect of our Lord Jesus Christ.

In this context, Origen says, "None of the evangelists announced the Lord's divinity as clearly as St. John. He is the one through whom the Lord says: " I am the Light of the world", " I am the Way, the Truth, the Life", " I am the Resurrection", " I am the Door", "I am the Good Shepherd." Moreover, we find in Revelations, "I am the Alpha and the Omega, the Beginning and the End, the First and the Last". In other words, this gospel presents to us the eternal relationship between the Father and the Son, as well as the implications of this unique relationship in the lives of believers and its role in their redemption. By revealing the Person of Jesus Christ as the only Son of God, St. John wishes us to believe in Him, become saved, and attain eternal life. The evangelist underlines that the Lord's contemporaries neither realised the full extent of His perfection nor the implications of His words nor deeds. That seemed to be beyond their comprehension. His blood relatives, such as His Mother, and His brothers (His cousins), His friends, the Jewish teachers, the priests, as well as the Samaritan woman and Pontius Pilate…all these did not comprehend His words and were astonished at His acts."

This idea is also revealed in the following contemplation:

I dare to say, dear brethren, that St. John himself did not speak of the issue in its entirety. Rather, he speaks insofar as he was able to comprehend. For he was a human being who spoke about God. It is true that God inspired him, yet remained a human being.

St. Augustine

Time and Place of Writing

According to the testimony of St. Irenaeus, Bishop of Lyon (177 A.D. - 200 A.D. approximately), who is a disciple of St. Polycarp, St. John delivered his Gospel to the bishops of Asia where he lived with them until the reign of Emperor Trajan. He had it published in Ephesus.

This testimony continues to be accepted in both the Eastern and Western Churches with hardly any opposition. However, some critics have recently raised doubts concerning the authority of St. John and consequently questioned the place and date of his writings.

Concerning the place of writing, some think it to be in Antioch, or Syria. They base their assumption on the information given in the Acts of Ignatius (being a document with an uncertain date), which mentions that St. John was closely bound to Antioch. The response to this is that St. John did stay in Antioch for a short time, but then he went to Ephesus where he resided for a long while.

Other critics believe it was written in Alexandria, and their claim to that is that the oldest manuscripts of St. John's Gospel have been found in Egypt. They also explain that the writing reflects a Hellenic style that corresponds to the thought of the School of Alexandria and that had been inspired by Philo, the Jewish Alexandrian thinker. The response to this theory, however, is that the academic climate of Egypt led the School to have it in its possession at a very early date. By having it at the School, the gospel could play a significant role in the life of her church and its fathers. This does not necessarily lead to the conclusion that it was written in Egypt.

Regarding the rejection of some critics to the testimony that the gospel was written in Ephesus, their view is based on the following two points:

1. Firstly, most of the recent critics confirmed during the first half of the twentieth century, that the style of writing of the Gospel of St. John is Gnostic and Hellenic. They say that it is a style that is not consistent with the first century after Christ, but instead belongs to the second century. Therefore, they insist that even if St. John was the one who wrote the original text, it had to have been rewritten by a Gnostic hand in Alexandria or Antioch during the second century. In 1947, the Manuscripts of the Dead Sea were discovered, as well as the complete Gnostic library found at almost the same time in Naga Hamadi, in Upper Egypt. These confirmed the opposite of what the critics insisted upon. Consequently, scholars withdrew and believed in the veracity of ecclesiastic tradition. Most of them became convinced that the gospel

of St. John was written in the first century and that St. John was most probably the one who wrote it while living in Ephesus. We will return to this subject when we later speak about "the Gospel of St. John and Gnosticism."

2. Secondly, some critics have tried to raise doubts concerning the belief that the gospel was written by St. John in Ephesus. They claim that Herod Agrippa the First, in Jerusalem, during the year 44 A.D, martyred the saint with his brother. They have presented evidence that can be refuted based on the following considerations, however:

a) In St. Mark's Gospel, chapter 10:39, the verse says that James and John would drink from the same cup as the Lord Jesus Christ. They claim that this means that John must have been martyred with his brother, otherwise St. Mark would have changed his version. The response to this is that St. Mark was obligated to report the exact words of the Lord Jesus Christ, and had no right to alter any of them, thereby leaving the interpretation to the reader. The Lord used the cup as a symbol to prophecy the sufferings that the two disciples were to undergo. It does not necessarily indicate martyrdom or the spilling of blood. Besides, if Herod had killed the two brothers together, St. Luke would not have mentioned the death of James only (in the book of the Acts of the Apostles). He would have mentioned both brothers, "Then he killed James the brother of John with the sword. And because he saw that it pleased the Jews, he proceeded further to seize Peter also" (Acts 12:2, 3).

b) The critics depended on a brief expression that occurs in the writings of two later authors: namely, Philip of Sidea, a writer of the fifth century, and George Hamartolus, who wrote in the ninth century. In their writings, they referred to Papayas who stated that the Jews had killed John and James. The response to their statements regarding that matter cannot be taken seriously since these two writers are known to be inaccurate historians. C.K. Barrett states that Irenaeus and Eusebius are acquainted with the writings of Papayas and that he does not mention anything about the martyrdom of St. John. Moreover, the fact that Philip of Sidea names St. John as the Divine, leads one to be suspicious since St. John was not known by that title in the days of Babias during the second century. Concerning what George Hamartolus has written, the matter was not taken seriously as he came back to the subject and reported that St. John had passed away peacefully (without martyrdom).

c) In the Syrian records of the Acts of the Martyrs in 411A.D., the commemorations of St. John and St. James are celebrated on the same day, i.e. December 27th. They are celebrated as two apostles from Jerusalem. This agrees with the Calendar of Carthage written in approximately 505A.D. However, some scholars point out the error that is made as the Baptist follows the name of St. John. Moreover, in the sermon of Fr. Avrahat, he states that we may add the names of John and James only to the names of Stephen, Peter, and Paul, as apostles who died as martyrs. The response to the above is that some confusion has occurred between St. John the Baptist and St. John the Apostle.

The following points also provide evidence that St. John did not die with his brother:

1. St. John is mentioned as one of the pillars of the Church in Galatians 9:2, and the date to that is after 44 A.D.

2. The archaeological finds of the Grave of St. John in Ephesus by Austrian scholars support the traditional ecclesiastic thought.

3. According to Polycrates, the Bishop of Ephesus had written to Victorianus, the Bishop of Rome, in approximately the year 190 A.D., to confirm that John the Apostle had lived in Ephesus and had died there. Concerning the date of the writing of the Gospel of St. John, it was penned towards the end of the apostle's life. This is based on ecclesiastical tradition. It is clear that it was written after the destruction of the temple of the Jews in Jerusalem in the year 70 A.D (refer to Jn 2:19, 20; 4:21). Thus, the writing took place probably during the period after the believers had been banned from the gatherings of the Jews around the years 85 to 90 A.D. (refer to Jn 9:22; 16:2).

The Lord preserved the life of this apostle and did not allow him to be martyred at an early time as the other disciples. It was His will that St. John would present to the young Church the Truth in a clear manner – the Gospel of St. John – and to lead her to the Day of the Lord so that

She could ultimately perceive the opened heavens and the Revelation of the Lord Jesus Christ.

We can learn more about the aim and significance of St. John's gospel through more contemplations from the Church Fathers:

Can't you see, it is not without a reason that we say, this Apostle is speaking to us from heaven? Just observe how, from the very beginning, he attracts the soul upwards and provides her with wings, and lifts up the minds of his hearers. In this manner, he lifts the soul above all that is tangible matter, and to heights above the earth and sky. He holds the soul's hands and leads her to heights that are above the Cherubim and Seraphim themselves, and even above thrones, authorities and powers. In a word, he urges her to go on a journey that transcends all creatures.

St. John Chrysostom

St. Paul's spirit was heaven-bound and he said, "For our citizenship is in heaven," (Phil 3:20). The same is true of St. James and St. John and therefore were called 'Sons of Thunder' (Mk 3:17). St. John was like someone who lived in heaven and consequently saw the Word of God.

St. Ambrose

HOW THE GOSPEL IS ARRANGED

St. John lived into the end of the first century and was the last one from among the Lord's disciples and apostles to leave this world. He lived to see a new generation of Christians, and he was – if we can correctly say so – the links between the Apostolic Era and the Post-Apostolic one. He wished to convey the final apostolic words about the nature of the Lord Jesus Christ, and to protect the Church from the invasion of wrong ideas.

Some scholars find that the Evangelist intended to face some of the Gnostic movements, such as Docetism, as these proclaimed that it is impossible for the Divine Word to become real flesh and incarnated. This was due to their perception of matter as being evil. Consequently, the Apostle ascertains in his gospel that Jesus is truly the Son of God and that He truly became incarnate. This was not fiction, for he says, "The Word became flesh." We could not have enjoyed redemption if He had not carried our nature in Him and actually shared our life. The Evangelist reinforces the presence of the Lord Jesus Christ in the wedding at Cana and how He takes on the role of everyone's servant. He turns the water into wine, a task that involves creation, yet He presents it as a humble service and does not expect to be given a seat of honour. At the well of Sikhar, the Lord appears tired and thirsty. At the tomb of Lazarus, He is overcome with grief and weeps. In the upper room He washes His disciples' feet, and on the Cross, He got thirsty.

The aim of this Gospel is to link the historical Jesus and the Lord who is present in His Church together. He used the events that occurred in the life of the Lord to proclaim His nature as the glorious God Who works in His Church.

MAIN THEMES IN THE GOSPEL OF ST. JOHN

The Gospel of St. John specifically achieves the 'fullness' of the Holy Bible; it is as though this Gospel represents the 'epicentre' of the mystery of the Bible. Fr. Maximus the Confessor likens the Holy Bible to the Holy Church and the Gospel of St. John as the Holy of Holies within her. Through St. John's Gospel, we enter into the sanctified depths of the Holy Bible, we become acquainted with its mysteries, and we break through the veil.

The 'Spiritual Gospel'

St. Clement of Alexandria justly calls it the 'Spiritual Gospel' that leads the soul to recognise the glories that have been prepared for her through the love of God the Father, the redeeming act of the Lord Jesus Christ, and the comfort of the Holy Spirit. St. Clement finds that the Gospel of St. John constitutes the spirit while the other three gospels constitute the body. The latter presents tangible facts and events in the life of the Lord Jesus Christ, His service and His redeeming work. The gospel of

St. John comes to present an interpretation of what lay behind these events and to reveal their depths and implications. Hence, the gospel is in harmony with the words of the Lord, "...that they may know You, the only true God, and Jesus Christ whom You have sent" (Jn 17:3).

This is the spiritual gospel since it raises the believer into the spiritual world. It does not allow him to remain on the material plane, "For when he had satisfied the multitudes with bread, they rejoiced (Jn 6:26), but He invited them to partake of the eternal food" (Jn 6:27).

We see more of this idea, that it is the spiritual gospel, through Christ's many conversations throughout the gospel of St. John. In the Lord's conversation with Nicodemus about the new Birth, the Jewish scholar's concept was limited to his own mother's womb. However, the Lord Jesus Christ raised him to see with his heart's vision that, "that which is born of the Spirit is spirit" (Jn 3:1-6).

Again, in the Lord's conversation with the Samaritan woman, we find that her thought is limited to her material bucket, Jacob's well, and his herds. However, Jesus lifts her heart to the Divine Source. From this, He offers her Water that will gush within her into sources of Living Water that flow into eternal life.

When St. John Chrysostom began to give sermons about the Gospel of St. John, he spoke about St. John, the evangelist. He presented his gospel and made a comparison between him, and the other speakers and actors. He explained how the latter attracted the masses by their skilful use of the language as well as music, and by parading in attractive masks. As for St. John the evangelist, he spoke as though he stood on a heavenly platform. Many of the people to whom he spoke had already become like angels; and he yearned that the rest of his listeners would be transformed likewise. He only armed himself with the Grace of God and considered himself in the company of the heavenly hosts. To these, St. John presented the joyful message of the Lord Jesus Christ. We can see this is St. John Chrystom's writing:

Now this man appears before us, the son of thunder, the beloved of the Lord Jesus Christ, the pillar of all Churches in the world, the one who holds the keys of heaven, who drank of the Lord's cup, was baptized by his Baptism and confidently leaned on his Lord's bosom...He entered wearing the robe of incomprehensible beauty, for he appears before us having put on the Lord Jesus Christ (Rom 13:14; Gal 3:27). His beautiful feet are shod with the preparation of the gospel of peace (Eph 6:15); and he is dressed not with a girdle around his waist but around his shoulders. His robe is not made of crimson hide, neither is it covered by gold on the outside. But it is woven and fashioned of the Truth Himself. Now St. John appears before us to head and proclaim openly the Truth. He does not appear wearing a mask and ready to play a theatrical role. He does not attempt to force the crowds to believe him, but rather uses gentleness and kindly looks and words to achieve his message without resorting to musical instruments such as the violin or similar objects. Indeed he only used his tongue and speaks with a voice that sounds sweeter and more effective than a harp or any other musical tool. His platform is all the heavens and his stage is the whole inhabited planet. His band consists of the angels. As for his hearers, they are human beings, many of whom are angels or wish to become likewise. These will not be able to enjoy fully his words unless they get transformed and demonstrate that change through their acts. As for the rest, they are like young children who hear yet do not understand... they are playful and leisurely and only live to possess wealth, power and sensual pleasures. What they hear is the Truth, yet their demeanor does not stress that which is great or noble since they hurry towards the earth that is used to make bricks.

He is no longer the fisherman and the son of Zebedee, for he is now the one who knows 'the deep things of God' (1 Cor 2:10), and of the Holy Spirit – by this I mean that he plays on that harp. Therefore, we wish we would listen to him. Note that he does not speak to us as a person in any way, for his words come from the depths of the spirit and from the mysteries that have not been revealed event to the angels. Indeed, the angels have learned about them from the voice of St. John and at the same time as we have. So they really got to know about matters through us and which we already knew. Another apostle explains this by saying, "...to the intent that now the manifold wisdom of God might be made known by the church to the principalities and powers in the heavenly places (Eph 3:10). Therefore, if the leaders, powers, cherubim and seraphim have learned these matters from the Church, it becomes clear that they are very eager to listen to these teachings. Indeed, we are granted such a great honour since the angels have learned about these things which they had not known before.   St. John Chrysostom

Introduction to
THE ACTS OF
THE APOSTLES

IN THE INTRODUCTION TO
THE ACTS OF THE APOSTLES, YOU WILL FIND

Introduction to the book

✳

About the author

✳

The purpose of the book

✳

How the book is arranged

✳

Main themes in the book

INTRODUCTION

This book presents the story of the Church at the beginning of its setting forth, after the ascension of the Lord Christ and the swelling of His Holy Spirit, along thirty years. St. Luke the Evangelist, inspired by the Holy Spirit, presented it to reveal to us the Church in the apostolic era. The secret of its birth, its growth, its worship, its testimony to the Lord Christ and its strength through the work of the Holy Spirit; and to reveal to us the realisation of the Lord's promise to His disciples, "I am with you always, even to the end of the age" (Matt 28:20). "But you shall receive power when the Holy Spirit has come upon you; and you shall be witnesses to Me in Jerusalem and in all Judea and Samaria and to the end of the earth" (Acts 1:8).

The book of the Acts of the Apostles is the book of the Church of Christ in the era that the apostles received His gospel and practiced it practically in her (the Church's) daily life, as well as in worship and preaching.

It is the gospel of the Holy Spirit who granted the Church the grace of existence on the day of Pentecost, received the Church of Christ to lead her, and to draw to her souls, that they may enjoy the Saviour granting her the persistent sanctity of life.

It is the book which the Church opens itself to the world, to minister to it and to wash its feet.

It is the book of the Church, poor and rich. She becomes poor with her Groom and becomes rich with Him.

It is the book of an inner strength that will never weaken or grow old.

It is the book of the Holy Church, who would never accept evil, yet she is compassionate to the sinner.

ABOUT THE AUTHOR

The Author, and Time and Place of Writing the Acts of the Apostles

The identity of the author is not mentioned in the book, but the tradition of the church confirms that its author is the Evangelist St. Luke. This view is supported by several testimonials within and outside the book.

Some believe that his book was written in Alexandria, although the majority of scholars believe that it was written in Rome whilst the apostle Paul was in prison, after St. Luke arrived there, together with St. Paul (Acts 28:16).

Many scholars believe that the Book of Acts was written about the year 63 A.D., when horrible acts of persecution were waged against the Christians, a little while after which St. Luke may have been martyred. As Rome was burnt, and the Christians faced slaying and burning, the appearance of the gospel according to St. Luke and the Book of Acts (as one book), was delayed, and did not actually occur until the seventy-year war came to an end (burning the temple by Titus) and the Church started to regain some freedom.

Some scholars have worked to support the opinion that the book was written before the year 63 AD, as shown through the following points:

1. St. Luke appears more interested in Jerusalem than the Evangelists, Matthew and Mark. He was called the 'travels narrator' (Luke 9.51, 16.15), having concentrated on the Lord Jesus' moves toward Jerusalem. His interest in the holy city is demonstrated in his narration of the events concerning the resurrection, concentrating on Jerusalem. If he had written the book after the events of the devastation of Jerusalem in the year 70 A.D., he would have mentioned that particular episode.

2. St. Luke recorded the troubles that faced the early Church, so he would not have disregarded the persecution by Nero in the year 64 A.D., when a huge number of Christians were martyred, including the two saints: Peter and Paul. This book must have been written before the devastating riot by Nero. Having mentioned the episodes of the

martyrdom of both James, son of Zebedee, and of Stephen, why should he disregard those of St. Peter and St. Paul?

3. The book presents the nature of Christian Theology in a primitive way, as to be expected in the time of the apostles. The theological language reveals, to a certain extent, the time of its writing. For example, calling the Christians 'disciples and referring to 'Sunday' as the first day of the week; beside the fact that the description of several incidents reveal that the author was an eyewitness, having a close relationship with the apostles, and one who lived in the atmosphere of the Church in the era of the apostles.

4. The tendency of the State toward the Church is another thing to consider. In this book, it is to be noticed that the Roman rulers and leaders did not persecute the Church, and in the few incidents it happened, it was provoked by the Jews. In some situations, the rulers even took the side of certain apostles, as that of St. Paul for example, whose life they saved from the plots planned by the Jews to kill him. That tendency was prevailing before the persecution of the Church by Nero in the year 64 A.D.

5. The Book of Acts did not mention the epistles of St. Paul and of other apostles; therefore, it must have been written before all those epistles

THE PURPOSE OF THE BOOK

The Aim of the Acts of the Apostles

The Evangelist gave us the goal of his gospel, which is an account of what Jesus had done and preached until the day of His ascension (Luke 1.1-4). Then, the Book of Acts carried out the same goal from the time of His ascension, all along the period of about thirty years. It was done to cover the work of the Lord Christ through His Church following His ascension as a record of the works of Christ, by His Holy Spirit, in His Church who testifies to Him, being the One working in her and who sent her His Holy Spirit.

"The Acts of the Apostles seem to relate a mere unvarnished narrative descriptive of the infancy of the newly born church; but when once we realize that their author is Luke the physician whose praise is in the gospel, we shall see that all his words are medicine for the sick soul."

HOW THE BOOK IS ARRANGED

The Acts of the Apostles in the New Testament

Until the end of the first century and the beginning of the second one, this book was considered to be a continuation of the gospel according to St. Luke, as the beginning of this book is written in harmony with the end of that gospel. Yet, after the gospel of St. John was written, the Church brought the four gospels together and this book came to form the connecting link that binds the four gospels and the epistles of the apostles together. As the epistles reveal the writings of the apostles, this book came to reveal their acts by the Holy Spirit of God, or the works of Christ in them, by them, and to their account. We could never have enjoyed the comprehension of those epistles as we should have, unless they are read through the background of this book. This book helps as well, in a living way, to study the bond between the teachings of the Lord Christ, and those of the apostles.

In some scripts, this book used to follow the epistles of the apostle St. Paul, since it presents the events pertaining to the ministry of St. Paul mentioned in his epistles.

The following is a comparison between the Acts of the Apostles, and the Holy Gospels:

1. While the gospels present to us the Lord Christ, being the Saving Messiah; the book of Acts reveals that the Messiah is present in His Church who anticipates His coming.

2. While the gospels present to us what the Lord Christ began to do for our sake; the book of Acts proclaims that He is still, with His Holy Spirit, present in His Church.

3. While the holy gospels talk about the Saviour who was crucified and resurrected from the dead, the book of Acts presents Him ascending to heaven – the glorified Lord and the leader of the Church.

4. While in the holy gospels we heard the teachings of the Lord Christ that bring us to salvation by His blood, the book of Acts allows us to come into touch with His salvation in His holy Church, to draw the nations to glory.

MAIN THEMES IN THE BOOK OF THE ACTS OF THE APOSTLES

Special Features of the Acts of the Apostles:

The 'Practical' Gospel

The Acts of the Apostles starts by the words of the evangelist, St. Luke, who writes, "The former account I made, O Theophilus of all that Jesus began both to do and to teach" (Acts 1:1). It is as though the four gospels are the 'former account,' pertaining to the works and teachings of the Lord; whereas this book is a consummation of that account. It is what the Lord began as He was present in the flesh on our land. He continues to do so by His Holy Spirit and His presence in the middle of His Church. The book reveals an important evangelical fact, that the Lord Christ, ascending to heaven, is alive, present, working and speaking in His Church and will continue to do so until the day of His ultimate appearance when his Church will be consummated, and will enjoy fellowship of His glory. The Book of Acts is a living gospel that testifies to the presence of Christ, working and speaking in His Church, through her, and to her account.

"And then, besides, there are doctrines to be found her, which we could not have known so surely as we now do, if this Book had not existed but the very crowning point of our salvation would be hidden, alike for practice of life and for doctrine."

St. John Chrysostom

The Book of the Acts of the Holy Spirit

This book presents the acts of the Holy Spirit, the Comforter, promised by the Lord to His disciples. We see Him behind the history of the Church, being the True Leader, the Guide and the Mentor, capable of drawing souls to experience the work of salvation by the Lord Christ. He shines with His light over the Church, to fill it, amid the afflictions, with a divine, hidden, and attractive splendor, to kindle the hearts with the divine fire of love. It is the divine river that flows from heaven, to set on earth the city of God, a fruitful divine paradise, in place of the barren, spiritually dry wilderness.

"The gospels are the history of what the Lord Christ has done and said; whereas, the book of Acts is an account of what the other Comforter has done and said. Yet, this Spirit has equally done many things that came in the other gospels; and Christ is still working as well in the book of Acts, in mankind, as He did in the gospels. There, he worked, as He came into the womb of the Virgin, as a temple; and now, He is working in the souls of the apostles. There, He came in the form of a dove, while here he comes in the form of fire."

St. John Chrysostom

The Book of the Rejoicing Church of the Crucified Christ

This book reveals the nature of the Church of the crucified Christ, since its beginning, having been formed by the Holy Spirit amid the affliction and bemoaning to bear the fellowship of passion and crucifixion, together with her suffering Groom. Yet, His presence in her midst transforms the bemoaning into a glorified joy, and the affliction into heavenly comfort, to let her live praising God amid the furnace of persecution.

It is fitting for the Christian to praise 'Alleluia', from head to toe.

Let us rejoice and give thanks; not because we became Christians, but because we became Christ. Do you realize that? Do you comprehend the magnitude of that great grace, granted to us by God? Let us then stand in awe and joy; we have become Christ!

"He who continually goes forth weeping, bearing seeds for sowing, shall doubtless come again with rejoicing, bringing his sheaves with him" (Ps. 126.6).

This psalm, which addresses the spirit of those who persist on going forth on their spiritual walk towards God, is very convenient in helping us during a time of grief and depression. This world is undoubtedly the valley of tears, where man sows while weeping. This psalm, however, encourages you to go forth in your faith.

St. Augustine writes about this, saying:

Anyhow, explaining what this book means by the seeds that we sow now, they are "the good works, which God prepared beforehand that we should walk in them" and has planned for us to practice by the power of His Spirit, amid the troubles of this disturbed life (Eph. 2.10).

Whoever is taught to practice the work of God in this world – the valley of tears and troubles – will rejoice like the diligent farmer who sows the seeds even during the death of winter. Can the cold wind and the severe weather hinder them from working? Certainly no!

That is how it is fit for us to look at the troubles of this world: Distractions will be put along our way by the evil one, in order to make us divert from the good works which God prepared beforehand that we should walk in them.

The Psalmist says, "He who continually goes forth weeping." Although each of us may actually find a reason for weeping; yet we should continue to go forth, practicing the good works of God that we should walk on.

How miserable we could be, if we are called to work diligently, only to weep without looking forward to some fruition of our work! How miserable we could be, if we find no one to wipe out our tears! But we know that the Holy Spirit works, to make us go forth on sowing amid our tears, as the Spirit promises us through the Psalmist that we shall come back amazed by joy. We shall bear the fruition of our labor, as an offering to Him.

St. Augustine

Spreading the Faith through Ministry

The realisation of the divine promise concerning the spreading of Christianity in Jerusalem, Judea, Samaria, and to the end of the earth (Acts 1.8), opens the gate of faith before all nations. This is counted by the Lord as the miracle of miracles, done by the Lord Jesus, by His Holy Spirit, through His disciples and apostles. The main factor in spreading the faith is the dwelling of the Holy Spirit, who granted the disciples the gift of talking in tongues to draw the Gentiles and to shut down the mouths of the fanatic Jews. It was also granted for the purposes of supporting the disciples with the capability of doing miracles and wonders in the name of Jesus Christ, guiding them and drawing the souls to the word.

Moreover, the heavenly hosts have taken part in the work; the angelic ministry appears mightily, to the account of the spreading of the kingdom of God through the Church. The Lord proclaimed to the disciples that they would be brought before governors and kings, and would be tried before Synagogues, for His sake (Matt. 10.18). Yet, that did not hinder the preaching in the whole world (Matt. 24.14).

It is a book of history and theology that brings to us to theological thought, through historical events, simply proclaiming that the Lord Christ is the Centre of history, and that the history of salvation is an integral part of the general history.

Although this book recorded for us the works of certain apostles like Peter, John, Paul, and others, it more so concentrated on the work of the Holy Spirit in them as a Leader and Organizer of the life of the early Church, and His work to spread the preaching to the end of the world. That is why once St. Paul arrived in Rome and testified of the Lord Christ in the capital of the Roman Empire (who at the time ruled the world), the book came to an end, with no reference to the martyrdom of St. Paul in the days of Nero. The goal of the book was that the preaching of salvation has gallantly reached even the palace of the Roman Emperor.

The Historical Continuity of the Acts of the Apostles

This book also reveals the continuity of God's goal by history. Even if the events that took place by Jesus Christ the Saviour of the world have entered history as historical events, that exalted divine work remains as "being delivered by the determined counsel and foreknowledge of God" (Acts 2.23). So also, are the events of preaching by the apostles, written in the Book of Acts. Although they are historical and temporal events, they testify to the continuation of the execution of God's plan in the world until the whole Church of Christ is realised to be worthy of the eternal inheritance and the fellowship of glory.

Its events are a realisation of prophecies that appeared in the Old Testament, done by the Holy Spirit Himself along the ages, up to the day of the ultimate coming of the Lord.

The Gospel of the Spirit

The book of Acts is also known as the Gospel of the Spirit. Because this book often refers to the Holy Spirit, it is apparent that its goal is not to tell about the troubles that the Church faced at the beginning of her setting forth, but to confirm that God by His Holy Spirit, is the guide of every movement in Her history. The growth of the Church was not actualised through the personal efforts of the apostles and the troubles that they encountered, as according to human thought, it was impossible for the world to accept the faith. But it is the fruit of God Himself, the lover of mankind, who works in the lives of the apostles, as well as of the people. The Holy Spirit grants the shepherds the strength and the talents to preach. He is the gift of God to his children in Baptism, granting them spiritual wisdom, and a word in the time of affliction (6,10). His talents are not acquired by money, like by Simonism (Acts 9). The power of the Holy Spirit is apparent in confronting the opponent Jews and giving the apostles power to stand before the rulers and kings. He is the stronghold surrounding the Church, and the secret of her strength and glory. And as it came in the book of Zechariah, "For I, says the Lord, will be a wall of fire all around her, and I will be the glory in her midst" (2,5).

St. Paul and St. Peter in the Acts of the Apostles

The apostle for the Gentiles, St. Paul, had his personality subject to harsh criticism. He was accused of being an opponent to Moses, "the Law," and his apostleship was even denied by some. It is a defence document that harmonises between the thoughts of Peter and Paul between the wish to gain the Gentiles, and the commitment to the law.

The two apostles were similar, as both of them healed the handicaps (Acts 3,14), the sick (Acts 5,18), were counted as sorcerers (Acts 8,13), raised someone from the dead (Acts 9,20), got out of prison through miracles (Acts 12,16), and went for three preaching trips. The similarity between both personalities has been magnificently and excitingly introduced, to confirm that St. Paul was an apostle on an equal level to St. Peter. Moreover, the book demonstrates certain situations of St. Peter, ministering to the Gentiles, and of St. Paul, keen on keeping the Law (Acts 16, 18).

The Book of Christian Teachings

It is a theological and didactic document, which includes 18 essays and speeches, constituting 25% of the book, most of which are an introduction to a living portrait of the teachings and theological thought of the early Church. We can say that the Book of Acts of the Apostles had introduced the seeds of the Christian creed, especially that of the salvation work of God, recognising God the Father, the Son Jesus Christ and the Holy Spirit, and their work in the life of the Church, as well as in the life of every believer as a living member in the Church. Yet, we cannot say that what came in the book is the complete program of all the teachings of the Church. Despite the harmony between what came in the book and what came in the epistles of the apostles, the epistles introduced in some detail the dogmas, the Christian teachings, and the behaviour fitting for the believer, in his personal life, in his home, in the Church and in the society in which he/she lives.

This book is also a guide for the Church, as it presents the main lines for the Church of the Lord Christ as a guide for her along the generations, in order to grow with no division, in the midst of affliction.

The evangelist St. Luke was not preoccupied by writing a record of the history of the early Church or parading a history of the apostles and their glorious works, but his goal was a preaching one. The book is a preaching work that proclaims salvation for everyone, wherever his location is, and whatever his circumstances may be. The Lord Christ Himself presents, through His Holy Spirit the salvation for all, with no discrimination. He presented His gospel to the Jew, as well as to the Greek or a Roman…to the man, as well as to the woman…to the rulers, governors, and leaders as well as to the mob…to the rich, as well as to the poor.

Introduction to THE PAULINE EPISTLES

IN THE INTRODUCTION TO THE PAULINE EPISTLES, YOU WILL FIND

Introduction and history

✳

About the author

✳

Audience and/or Author of the Epistle

✳

Purpose of the Epistle

✳

Main themes and structure of the Epistle

Introduction to
THE EPISTLE TO
THE ROMANS

INTRODUCTION AND HISTORY

Some scholars indicate that the word 'Rome' has a Greek origin denoting 'power;' and that it was used to convey 'go safely,' which implies 'may you have sound health.' Others note that the word means 'an elevation.' The city could have been given this name for two reasons: firstly, it was named after Romulus who founded the city in the year 753 B.C. and so it carried his name. Secondly, the name was inspired by its construction on one of the high elevations of the seven mountainous ranges of that area. Eventually, the city expanded and covered the other six neighbouring ranges. In the middle of the sixth century, a wall was constructed around the whole city, in spite of its huge scale. The circumference of the wall was five miles and it had 19 'Roman' gates.

The scope and power of Rome spread so that it became the capital of the Roman Empire, which had captured all the lands bordering the Mediterranean Sea. The city grew so big that houses were built outside the city walls as well. Eventually, Rome became the meeting place for world politicians and rulers, and the learning centre for the Sciences, Arts, and Philosophy. It became especially famous for the Roman law, which is still being taught in most universities today around the world. As the city welcomed people from all over the world, Rome became infiltrated with controversial and immoral idolatry practices...this is clearly apparent from the content of Chapter One in the Epistle to the Romans.

In the first century, the population of Rome was 2 million approximately, although this estimate is considered an exaggeration. A third of that population consisted of immoral people. The inhabitants were mostly of varied origins and nationalities. There was also a big number of Jews who were brought captive by the great warrior of Pompeii when he seized Syria in the year 63 BC, and whom he allowed to live in one part of the city. These Jews eventually were set free, and their numbers grew and reached sixteen thousand approximately at the time of St. Paul the Apostle. They existed peacefully and comfortably most of the period they lived in Rome; except in the year 19 A.D. during the reign of Tiberius. Later on, in the year 34 A.D., during the reign of Claudius Caesar, he gave an order to expel them all from Rome (Acts 18:2). An indication of their great number is evident when a committee of Jews came to Rome, when Herod the Great died. They had come to seek the favour of Augustus Caesar. At that time, about eight-thousand of the wealthiest Jews in Rome came out to greet them. The Jews had more than thirteen Councils and were generally inclined to arouse divisions and rebellions.

The Establishment of Christianity in Rome

There is no mention in the New Testament about the birth of the Church in Rome. Moreover, the person who first carried the torch of faith to this city is unknown. However, we observe the following concerning the birth of Christianity in this area:

1. In the Acts of the Apostles, we are told that devout Jews from every nation came to Jerusalem on the day of the Pentecost...among them were 'visitors from Rome, both Jews and proselytes...' (Acts 2). During their visit they accepted the faith and believed in the Lord Jesus Christ. Consequently, when they left Jerusalem and returned to Rome, they preached among their Jewish fellowmen. Based on that, many scholars

consider that the Church of Rome, in its early days and until the writing of St Paul's Epistle to the Romans, was made up of members who were mostly of Jewish origin. This explains why the Epistle is directed to the triumphant converted Jews more than to the triumphant converted Gentiles. As a result of this situation, the Roman leaders assumed that the Christians were just a Jewish sect that had chosen to be separate from the rest of the Jews.

2. The Roman Empire was characterised by freedom and the ease to travel, especially from one part of the country to the capital. Rome had become the centre where the big leaders, scholars, and traders gathered. There is no doubt that many of these were Christians who were originally Jews or Gentiles. They came with their hearts filled with the fervent faith and they preached and witnessed for the Lord Jesus Christ. Among them were those who had listened and accepted the teachings of St. Paul as he preached in the Aegean cities, in Macedonia and other areas of Greece and Asia Minor. This is confirmed by the greetings St. Paul sends in the last chapter of the epistle where he mentions many of their names. It also reveals that he knew them and that they were his disciples, even though he had not visited Rome before the writing of the Epistle to the Romans.

3. The emperor, Claudius, had issued an order to expel many of the Jews, or possibly all of them, from Rome. As a result, many went to other cities, though they soon returned to the city again. Some of those had become believers in the Lord Jesus Christ, such as Priscilla and Aquila, who had met St. Paul in Corinth (Acts 18:1, 2). Through him, they learned about the faith, and he used to join them in making tents…these and others like them actively participated in establishing the Church in Rome (Rom 16:5).

4. It is clear from the epistle that none of the disciples had established a Church in Rome up to the time of its writing. St. Paul expressed his principle on that issue as he says, "And so I have made it my aim to preach the Gospel not where Christ was named, lest I should build on another's foundation," (Rom 15:20). In the same epistle, he speaks of his enthusiasm to go to Rome and how he had been hindered from doing so a number of times. He finally decided to go there, and this

confirmed that none of the disciples had visited Rome before him (Rom 1:9, 19; 15:22-24).

5. St. Paul felt he was the commissioned messenger to the Gentiles (Gal 2:7,11). He therefore felt a responsibility towards this city, as it was the centre of the Gentiles world at that time. He also sought to make it one of the centres of his ministry since he felt indebted to preach to them.

6. Most western and eastern scholars find it hard to agree with the claim that St. Peter the apostle is the one who established this Church and occupied the papacy seat in Rome for 25 years. Actually, St. Peter was present in Jerusalem up to the time when the Apostolic Council met in the year 50 A.D., approximately (Acts 15). In 55 A.D., he was in Antioch where he met St. Paul (Gal 2:11). If he was in Babylon when he wrote his first epistle in 60 A.D. as some claim, then St. Paul would not have undertaken to write this epistle to the Romans. Or if he had written it, he would not have said that he would not preach the gospel where Christ had already been preached, lest he should build on another's foundation, and he would have mentioned St. Peter's name or sent him greetings.

AUDIENCE OF THE EPISTLE TO THE ROMANS

Time and Place of Writing

The apostle wrote this epistle while he anticipated his visit to Rome. He had made the decision to stop there on his way to Spain (Rom 15:23,24). This would take place after he had gone to Jerusalem, where he delivered the donations from the Christians of Macedonia and Achaia to the poor in Jerusalem (Rom 15:25,26; 1 Cor 16:1-16; 2 Cor 8:1-4). Therefore, the epistle was written during his third missionary journey to Corinth, and in the house of a man called Gaius. St. Paul describes him as his "host and the host of the whole Church" (Rom 16:23). Gaius is one of two whom the apostle St. Paul had baptised.

The apostle had dictated the epistle to Tertius, (Rome 16:22), and it was Phoebe, the deaconess, who carried it to Rome. She was a servant in the Church in Cenchria, (Rom 15:1). This was a port in the west of Corinth.

St. Paul had gone to Jerusalem in the spring of 58 A.D. Therefore, most scholars consider that the Epistle was written between 57 and 58 A.D.

The Members of the First Church in Rome

It would be impossible to comprehend the aim of this epistle and perceive the depth of its significance, unless we become acquainted with those who were members of the early Church in Rome and to whom it was directed by. Were they Jews who had triumphantly become Christians? Were they Gentiles who had accepted the faith? Or were they a mixture of both?

Proponents of the first opinion represent the school of thought led by Tubingen, E. Renan, T Zahn, W Manson and Leenhardt. They believe that the greater part of the members were triumphant converted Jews. They support this view by pointing out that the apostle used many quotations from the Old Testament, specifically, relating the story of Abraham to whom he called 'our father.' The reader therefore gets the sense that the apostle most commonly directed his discourse to those of Jewish origin. Besides, in the first century, the Jewish population in Rome was significantly large.

Proponents of the second opinion are J Munck, S Lyonnet, O Michel and C K Barett. They claim that the vast majority of the members were originally Gentiles. They base their opinion upon the belief that St. Paul's words are directed to them as he considered himself to be the messenger to the Gentiles, (1:5-7, 12-14; 11:11-13, 15:16). They indicate that St. Paul compares them with those from other Gentile nations (1:12-14). In his address to them, he says, "…you presented your members as slaves to uncleanliness and lawlessness…" (6:19). These words apply to those of Gentile origin, rather than to those of Jewish origin. He also addresses them by saying, "I speak to you Gentiles…" (11:13).

The third opinion belongs to a mixture of the above two groups who were led by Headlam, Sanday and Dodd.

Based on the above, we may conclude that the Church included both converted Jews and Gentiles, although those of Jewish origin greatly outnumbered the others.

PURPOSE OF THE EPISTLE

The Aim of the Epistle to the Romans

This Epistle is of great significance in the history of the early Church. It is said that St. John Chrysostom used to read it twice per week.

A study of the Epistle will enable us to comprehend its importance, and to discover from its contents the reasons that led to its writing, including its contemporary setting where a significant number of the Jewish Romans had become believers in the Lord Jesus Christ. These were either of a Hebrew origin or were Gentile converts. Besides these, there were some educated heathen Gentiles who were Greek scholars and had come to believe in the Lord. All these needed to meet together in one spirit and as members in one Body. However, the Jews were unable to easily dismiss their feelings of superiority over the rest even though they had all converted into Christianity. Due to their uncompromising conservatism and strong adherence to their race, culture, and religious teachings, they belittled the converted Gentiles. They felt they were superior based on the following claims:

1. They were the children of Abraham, therefore the heirs to the promise made to his descendants.

2. They were the recipients – chosen out of all other people, to receive the Law of Moses.

3. They alone were God's chosen people.

This manner of thinking, which they maintained from their Jewish past, led to an embedded pride that hindered them from understanding neither the meaning of being Abraham's children, nor the ultimate aim of the Law, nor of God's purpose in choosing His people. Consequently, even after they had accepted the belief in the Messiah as Saviour, they still believed they occupied a higher rank above all other believers.

On the other hand, and as a reaction to this Jewish concept, some converted Gentiles adopted a counter attitude. They regarded the Jews as an ungrateful nation, and that the door had been shut in their faces only to be widely opened to the Gentiles. This made them just as guilty of pride as the Jews.

MAIN THEMES ANFD STRUCTURE OF THE EPISTLE TO THE ROMANS

<u>Teaching Practical Faith and Removing Pride</u>

In these circumstances, the Epistle of St. Paul was written and directed to both parties. It intends to handle the practical implications of faith and spiritual behaviour in daily life. These would affect Church life throughout generations to come. The Apostle discusses in his Epistle the message of salvation in its widest implications. He proclaims that the door has been opened to all nations through a living faith that is evident in deeds of love. Inspired by the Holy Spirit, the Apostle presents the meaning of faith and its close relation to salvation. He also reveals his apostolic heart that is greatly charged with love for the Messiah and for the whole world for which the Lord was crucified. At the same time, St. Paul deals with the problem of pride, which threatens the lives of both Jews and Gentiles. He addresses the issues of sanctification, living faith evident in general relationships and compassion towards weak members, and the interactions of a believer in society. Indeed, this Epistle has been described as "the cathedral of the Christian faith." St. Paul's message leads the believer into the presence of the sublime holiness of God, and elevates him--through the altar of applied and living faith--to meet the heavenly Father through the action of the sacrificial Son and by the work of the Holy Spirit.

The Gospel of St. Paul

Some consider that this Epistle has been written to confront the supporters of the 'Judaic movement', which called believers to return to the literal application of the Law. This dictated observing circumcision, purification, seasonal cleansing, and the enforcement that Gentiles convert to Judaism before baptism. Others consider that this Epistle has been written to reconcile both parties--converted Jews and converted Gentiles. However, the Apostle St. Paul has not delivered his Epistle in a defensive manner, nor intended it merely as an instrument of reconciliation. Rather, he has intended it as a message, which elaborates on the faith of the Church, presenting with utmost precision the implications of an evangelical and saintly life. Therefore, this Epistle has been described as the 'Gospel of St. Paul'.

One of the objectives of this Epistle was to announce St. Paul's intention to visit Rome. He had made many attempts to go there, so this was a message to prepare for his visit and for his aim to preach the gospel of the Lord Jesus Christ there. The early Church had now accepted the new perception of proclaiming that the doors of salvation have been opened to all nations and Gentiles. Therefore, St. Paul was preparing the path so that when he would visit Rome, he would not get into conflict with the narrow-minded promoters of Judaism. He might have been driven to write this Epistle after receiving news from his disciples and acquaintances concerning the Church in Rome. This could have led him to write and seek solutions before his upcoming visit.

Introduction to
THE FIRST
EPISTLE TO THE
CORINTHIANS

INTRODUCTION AND HISTORY

The city of Corinth was a prominent Greek city 40 miles west of Athens. Its history goes back to the year 1000 B.C., when some of the ancient tribes settled down in it. The old Corinth was so famous in the Hellenic world, that it was labelled, 'The Rich Corinth' by Homer, and 'The light of all Greece' by Ciceron. In the year 800 B.C., it was known as a huge industrial city, particularly in shipbuilding, to which Thucydides noted that the first military ship in the world was built in Corinth during the year 664 B.C.

Located across a land strait between two seas (the Aegean and the Adriatic Seas), Corinth had two harbours: Cenchreae and Lechaem. What made this city so important, was where it was located on the land highway that connected the east from the west, binding Rome--the capital of the Roman world at the time--to the east.

Corinth was known as a city that was very open to the world, and not just as the most famous commercial city, but also for holding biennial sport game competitions in the Isthmus of Corinth. These competitions were second to, if not, the same level as, the Olympic Games.

In the year 146 B.C., however, it was destroyed by the Roman forces led by Mummius, who killed the men and took its women and children as captives. Corinth was then rebuilt by Julius Caesar in the year 46 B.C., when Greece separated from Macedonia. It was then that Corinth became the capital of the province of Achaia and the seat of the Roman governor, on behalf of the Roman congress and not of the Roman emperor. It kept its good economic fortune, until it fell under Turkish rule in the year 1485 A.D.

Corinth's Licentiousness

Having been an open city, Corinth embraced several religions. Groups of Jews came to it after being expelled from Rome by Claudius Caesar, including Aquila and Priscilla (Acts 18:2); as well as Jews from Palestine, for doing business, or as slaves purchased by its inhabitants. Several Egyptian, Roman and far-eastern gods were worshipped there too, beside Aphrodite, the Greek goddess of beauty and love whose temple was built high up on its top. Over time, Corinth became an example for licentiousness, with about 1000 heathen priestesses being dedicated to harlotry to the account of the temple, so much so, that new terms were added to the Greek language: 'Koine Corinthacin" to mean (live Corinthian), or (live corrupt); 'A Corinthian girl' to mean (a Corinthian harlot) ; To live a Corinthian, to mean (to be Corinthianised) or to (plunge in corruption). The Aphrodite worship goes back to a Phoenician origin.

The city of Corinth, known by the apostle St. Paul, was partly destroyed in the year 521 A.D. by an earthquake, and was then later utterly destroyed by another earthquake in the year 1858 A.D. The modern Corinth was rebuilt four kilometres far from the old city.

AUDIENCE OF THE EPISTLE

The Establishment of the Christian Church in Corinth

The Christian church in Corinth was founded by St. Paul during his second preaching trip (Acts 18). There, his ministry over the period of 28 months (51 to 52 A.D.), was very successful, despite the corruption that prevailed in the city. This was the longest time spent by the apostle anywhere after Ephesus.

Starting his ministry in Corinth among the Jewish society and the proselyte Gentiles, the apostle Paul presided with Aquila and Priscilla, with whom he worked as a tentmaker (Acts 18:3-10). During this time, we drew to the Christian faith Crispus, the ruler of the Synagogue and all his household (Acts 18:8). However, the opposition of the Jews was so fierce that he shook his garment and said to them, "Your blood be upon your own heads; I am clean; From now on I will go to the Gentiles" (Acts 18:4-6). He departed from there and entered the house of a certain man named 'Justus,' where a Church was established that embraced many.

At the beginning of his ministry in Corinth, the apostle was so shocked by the horrible atmosphere of corruption, aside from the fierce conflict between the different categories of inhabitants coming from several countries for business, that he had the intention to go back to Thessalonica (1 Thessalonians 2:17-18). However, his plans were utterly changed by a divine proclamation (Acts 18:9-20), by which God commanded him to stay in Corinth and testify boldly.

To the apostle, Corinth was especially important, as it was the greatest of Greek cities at the time. He considered the success of ministry in it as a symbol of its success in the Gentile world, particularly among those with a philosophical mind, who used to boast of their cultural prominence, proclaim slogans like knowledge and freedom, and at the same time, practice the corrupt pagan life. The successful ministry there reveals the rich work of God's grace in sanctifying the corrupt who throw themselves into the bosom of God.

It seems that the Church in Corinth gained a significant number of low-level people within the society, particularly the slaves (7: 21; 1: 26); beside some elites like Titus and Justus (11:21-22). The city at that time embraced 200,000 free citizens and 400,000 slaves.

The apostle Paul also managed to bring to the faith a multitude of souls among traders, sailors, professional wrestlers and gamblers, and those dedicated to corruption of both sexes and slaves. They came from Rome, Greece, Egypt and Asia Minor, and with such a diversity of races, cultures, financial possibilities and religious backgrounds. They were required to submit to the Spirit of God, who sanctifies them and grants them the spirit of unity and harmony, as Church holy to the Lord Jesus.

After departing from the city, someone by the name of 'Apollos' came to it. He was an Alexandrian Jew with high Hellenic culture, who received the Christian faith and preached it. Although his ministry in Corinth was fruitful (3:5-9), his name was abused by some to stir-up controversies in the Church. Some claimed to be followers of Paul, the first preacher in the city, others to be followers of the apostle Peter, probably for having been baptised in Palestine on his hands, beside their belief that he was faithful in keeping the literal Jewish law. A fourth group who counted themselves as followers of Christ, likely wishing to be free of commitment to any human leadership and to do whatever they like. By that, however, they misunderstood the spirit of Christian freedom.

Many scholars believe that the apostle Paul visited Corinth three times at least.

The Authenticity of the Epistle

In his four epistles, the first and the second to the Corinthians, the one to the Galatians and that to the Romans, Paul the apostle to the Gentiles, recorded a great apologetic thesis for the sake of receiving the Christian faith by the Gentiles; all of which go back to his third preaching trip during which a multitude of new believers from many nations were drawn to Christian belief on the apostle's hands. Some consider these four epistles to be the most important of his writings, with some even calling them 'the great epistles' or 'the four main epistles.' These epistles were bearing the apostle's wide-range of thoughts that set forth across humanity. From death to the life-giving Spirit, St. Paul's heart was wide open before everyone with no partiality, and within his depths, he yearned for the salvation of all men.

Both the first and second epistles to the Corinthians are referenced to the writings of the apostle Paul without any doubt, based upon the following 'external' and 'internal' testimonies:

The 'External Testimonies

• These two epistles occupy a prominent position among the oldest lists of writings from the apostle Paul. In the Muratorian Canon (in about the year 170 A.D.), these two epistles came at the top of the nine epistles directed to the Churches; with a statement that they were written to counter the contentions resulting from heresies.

• In the writings of Marcions Apostolicon (in about the year 140 A.D.) they came directly after the epistle to the Galatians.

• St. Clement the Roman (in about the year 95 A.D.), who was a friend of the apostle Paul (Philippians 4:3), referred to the contents of these two epistles in a message to the Corinthians, asking them to commit themselves to the directions of the apostle Paul concerning the contentions in the Church.

• St. Ignatius of Antioch, St Polycarp and St Justin the Martyr, referred to them as well.

The 'Internal' Testimonies

• The two epistles are packed with inside signs that confirm their authenticity as being referred to the apostle Paul. Although they both bear amazing harmony and conformity with the 'The Acts of the

Apostles' written by St. Luke the Evangelist, it could not be said that either of them quoted from the other, as the two epistles and the book of Acts each have distinctive traits that separate one from the other.

• There is no way to doubt the epistles' reference to Paul the great apostle, as he bears a compassion and flaring zeal for the salvation of souls, and with the overall multitude of preaching travels he practiced.

• As an example, when he talked about the five hundred witnesses who saw Christ risen from the dead, most of whom were still alive at the time this epistle was written, he was telling them the episode of the resurrection in the era of the apostles, which seemed to be something ridiculously funny in the sight of non-believers.

Important Events of the Church in Corinth and the Trouble they Experienced

The majority of the members of the Church in Corinth were Gentiles (12:2), together with a decent number of Jews, whose fathers the apostle called "Our fathers" (10:1-11).

Besides suffering from general controversies, the Church was under the great pressure of the corruption that prevailed in the city, including idol worship, sorcery, connection to evil spirits, and licentiousness. Some women rebelled against the custom of wearing a head cover, used by honorable ladies; some men intended to grow their hair, some women used to raise their voice in the Church while talking to their men, in an attempt to show off their social prominence; some misunderstood the significance of speaking in tongues, thus create an atmosphere of chaos in the Church that led to the apostle writing down in this epistle that,"God is not the author of confusion but of peace" (14:33); also adding, "Let all things be done decently and in order" (14:40).

According to St John Chrysostom, "The city was packed with speakers and philosophers, among whom was 'Periander' who was considered as one of seven most wise men of his time." Talking about the result of such a situation, the saint says, "Seeing how such a great city has received the truth and eagerly listened to the world of God, the devil planned to divide them apart, with knowledge that once a kingdom divided on itself; it would not stand. To do that he had the right weapon in the haughtiness and the boasting wisdom among its inhabitants."

Some counted themselves better than others, some abused their freedom by eating the meat of sacrifices ordered to idols and doing this even in the idol temples, causing a controversy in the Church. Some, for the sake of profiting, sued their brethren in civil courts. Some men let their hair grow, some others ate in the Church while completely disregarding fellowship with the needy. Some boasted of having spiritual gifts, causing dissension in the Church, and others still rejected the teaching of the resurrection of Christ. All of these things resulted from the influence of the evil pagan philosophy that caused dissention, even among the philosophers themselves.

Apart from all of these things, a particularly serious crime was committed during this time, being that some of prominence within the city, sinned with his father's wife. However, this man disregarded the rebuke and even became a leader of the people. Theodore, Bishop of Cyprus, says that, "The Church was divided into several groups, each with leaders, eloquently defending their doctrines, and entering into debates against the other groups. One of them who dared to have a sinful relationship with their father's wife, was admired because of his eloquence."

THE PURPOSE OF THE FIRST EPISTLE
TO THE CORINTHIANS

The Aim of the First Epistle
to the Corinthians

The apostle Paul departed from Corinth after 18 months of a very successful and fruitful ministry. As soon as he left, however, the established Church fell through a succession of events that led to a serious dissension, resulting in the appearance of four adversary groups inside the Church. Besides certain behavioural and doctrine problems that threatened to deprive the Church of her holiness and to destroy her faith, there were some things that made the apostle very uncomfortable, which included the following:

1. Having been distressed by a letter he received from Chloe's household, telling him about serious contentions among the congregation (1:11), the apostle sent out his disciple, Timothy, to Corinth for the sake of reconciliation, providing him with many commandments (4:17; 16:10). However, it is likely that the epistle within our hands arrived there before he did.

2. Having received a report concerning the already mentioned act of sexual immorality, the apostle felt commitment to send them an epistle to warn them against having a fellowship with a person; which is lost so far.

3. A certain message from Corinth to the apostle, lost as well, was probably the main reason for writing the epistle that we now have today.

The Church then turned into numerous controversial groups, whose voices were raised without limit. While some members of the congregation led a life of licentiousness and disorder, others sued their brethren in heathen courts. Many controversial views appeared concerning matrimonial and family relationships as a whole (7); concerning the banquets and food offered to the idols (8-10); the behaviour of some women in the meetings, and in the banquets of love of the Lord (11); the abuse of spiritual gifts (12-14); the hope in the resurrection of the dead (15) and concerning the collection for the saints in Jerusalem (16).

Aside from the problems causing contentions in the Church, there were also certain theological (doctrine), ethical, social, worship and eschatological problems. There were people who cared for the theoretical philosophies and human wisdom, more than for the working and living faith. As such, the main topic of this epistle came to be about "Our Lord Jesus Christ", shifting the main attention away from everything else and back onto Christ.

MAIN THEMES AND STRUCTURE OF THE FIRST EPISTLE TO THE CORINTHIANS

Special Features of the First Epistle to the Corinthians

The Book of Practical Faith

The epistle, presenting such clear and readily received solutions of faith, firmly and seriously condemns every fault, corruption or diversion of faith. It takes away doubts and supports faith. It presents to all the spirit of exalted compassion and true love, through the divine truth and the work of God's grace. Although this epistle mostly presents deep insight and thought, it also cared for the practical life of faith. It also came written in such an exalted order, that its reader would find no difficulty in following the author, moving from point to another

The Importance of Doctrine

The epistle presents to us important information concerning the doctrine. Specifically, it discusses and clarifies the Christian understanding of the two Persons of Christ and the Holy Spirit, the Eucharist, and the Resurrection. It also reveals the nature of the Church meetings and ministry of the early Church, ensuring to underline the major faults and evils practiced by the believers who recently came to the faith from idol worship. By highlighting the shortcomings that were present within the Church of Corinth, St. Paul wrote to demonstrate that the gospel satisfies all aspects of life. He focuses the importance of the gospel on the foundations by which believers were mostly committed to, such as family life, relationships with others, worship, behaviour in the markets and while having leisure time or under temptations. With all of this, the believers would lead a life of harmony, knowing nothing but Jesus Christ and His crucifixion.

The Power of the Cross

One of the main features of the epistle is demonstrating the power of the cross, being the power of God and His wisdom for salvation. It reveals the dynamic power to change the foundations of the inner man and to renew his depth, which is to change the life of the old pagan world. The work of preaching salvation was not done by Paul, by Apollos or by Safa (Peter); but was done by the preaching of the crucified Christ.

The apostle Paul put the cross very high up, to cast its shadow on all the activities of human life and on all aspects. The cross for him is not anguish or deprivation, but it is the foundation of the opening of the heart and the mind with love, and the enjoyment by the believers of eternal glory.

The Corinthians were used to practicing Greek democracy. The students would listen to the teachers, not to learn, as much as to offer commendation, criticism or reproach. They carried all that with them into the church, as well as the spirit of struggle and of competition, which they also practiced in the sport tournaments held in Corinth. The apostle Paul in this epistle dealt with everything that came to his knowledge in the reports he received.

He presents to us the judgments on several aspects:

1. Judging others (5:5)

2. Judging ourselves (11:31)

3. Our judgment by the Lord (11:32)

4. Judgment of the brethren (6:5)

5. We shall judge the world (6:2)

6. We shall judge angels (6:3)

7. Judgment before worldly courts (6:6)

Introduction to THE SECOND EPISTLE TO THE CORINTHIANS

INTRODUCTION AND HISTORY

The Book of Ministry and Guidance

The second epistle to the Corinthians is the most prominent essay within the Bible concerning the concept of ministry and the shepherding love of Christ. Every phrase is considered to be a practical law for the true minister. It is as though God allowed for the attack on the apostleship of St. Paul to make him reveal the depths of his love toward his people, and to share his thoughts on the true concepts of faith and the meaning of shepherding.

Despite the multitude of difficulties and problems that confronted the apostle in Corinth, the subject of this epistle came to deal with "The triumphant canonical ministry." "Thanks be to God who always leads us in Triumph in Christ" (2 Corinthians 2:14).

The intense afflictions that confronted the apostle did not destroy his soul, because he realised that they were allowed by God to reveal His hand working in the midst of troubles, "Who also made us sufficient as ministers of the new covenant, not of the letter but of the Spirit; for the letter kills, but the Spirit gives live" (2 Corinthians 3:6).

AUDIENCE OF THE EPISTLE

Time and Place of Writing

The second epistle to the Corinthians was written in the year 57 A.D. and was sent from Macedonia a few months after the first epistle.

PURPOSE OF THE SECOND EPISTLE TO THE CORINTHIANS

The Aim of the Second Epistle to the Corinthians

Some Jews came from Jerusalem to create doubt in the apostleship of Paul, claiming that he is aggressive in his epistles but weak in his presence. Unfortunately, some of the Corinthians listened to them and started to deny his apostolic authority. Paul found it necessary, therefore, to prove the authenticity of his apostleship (Chapters 1 to Chapter 7 and(Chapter 10 to Chapter 13), confirm his love for his people and his readiness to be their servant, so that they would enjoy the liberty of the glory of being children of God (4:5). St. Paul writes that "he will very gladly spend to be spent for their souls; though the more abundantly he loves them, the less he is loved" (12:15). He has already proclaimed to them that he would be inflamed within the depths of his heart, should any of them stumble, and would feel weak if any of them is weak (11:29).

Being informed by Titus that his first epistle to them had a positive response and fruition of true repentance (7:16), the apostle is thus writing in his second epistle to confirm his joy for their repentance and that his heart is wide with love for them. St. Paul notes that he is content, as well, upon hearing that the affairs of the Church have been put in order and that the faults have been gradually corrected. In this epistle, he is writing to encourage them to keep going along this sound path.

Ambrosiaster believes that St. Paul wrote this epistle for the sake of a few of them who stubbornly kept reverting back to their wrong ways. Although the epistle was very mild, at its end, he needed to be very firm due to the persistence of a few of them in denying his apostleship and resisting the ministry.

What made him hasten to write this epistle, was because of a person whom he had previously commanded to be separated. This was due to the evil he committed with his father's wife (1 Corinthians 5). However, having truly repented his sin, and genuinely grieved, the apostle feared that he might fall into despair again, and so hastened to write to them to receive him back with all possible love (2:7). He also wrote to thank them because of their care for the persecuted brethren in Jerusalem and for their good reception of Titus while visiting them (8:9).

MAIN THEMES AND STRUCTURE
OF THE SECOND EPISTLE TO THE CORINTHIANS

The topics dealt with in the two epistles to the Corinthians are almost identical; namely, the spiritual gifts, the resurrection from the dead, the Lord's supper, the exhortation to give abundantly (9:1-15), and love (1 Corinthians 13).

He wrote to warn them against heresies and contention, and to tell them about the divine comforts granted by God to His believers in the midst of sufferings. The apostle had to make a comparison between the Old and the New Covenants, not to belittle the importance of the law, but to respond to the few Christians of Jewish origin who persisted in accusing him of apostasy and resistance to the law.

In his first epistle he promised to visit them (1 Corinthians 16:5), but as he could not fulfill his promise, on account of being preoccupied by the Spirit with more important tasks, he is writing his second epistle to apologise to them for his delay. According to St. John Chrysostom, he did not promise to visit them, but he rather revealed his wish to do that.

Introduction to THE EPISTLE TO THE GALATIANS

INTRODUCTION AND HISTORY

Jesus the Liberator

The epistle of St. Paul to the Galatians portrays our Saviour as our Liberator. He made us free (5:1) and granted us a new concept of freedom.

The epistle written by St. Paul is ascertained by St. Ignatius of Antioch, Polycarp, and Justin. It is explicitly attributed to St. Paul by St. Irenaeus and already found in the Muratorian Canon and in all the catalogues drawn by the earliest councils. Moreover, the internal evidence reveals itself in every line by the unique hand and personality of St. Paul.

AUDIENCE OF THE EPISTLE

Time and Place of Writing

Scholars do not agree upon the specific identity of the Galatians, the people to whom St. Paul wrote this letter to. Looking at a map of the ancient world doesn't help either, as the map was changed often.

The Galatians by race were Celts, who had settled in the centre of the Asia minor during the third century B.C. There are a few theories concerning this:

The North Galatian theory

According to this theory, the letter was addressed to the Galatians by race, or to the Churches located in the old kingdom of Galatia i.e. in the north central part of Asia Minor (Pessinus, Ancyra and Tavium). During St. Paul's second missionary journey (Acts 16:6), he was delayed in Galatia by sickness (4:13). Though ill, the tireless servant of the Lord could not remain silent, and so continued to preach the gospel. As such, he succeeded in founding the Christian Churches in Galatia (1:6). According to this theory, the letter was written between 53 and 57 A.D. from Ephesus or Macedonia.

The South Galatian theory

After the death of its king, Ayntas, in 25 B.C., Rome combined the section with southern territories into one province named Galatia. Some scholars state that the epistle was actually written to the communities founded on Paul's first missionary journey in the area of Asia Minor, extending from the seacoast inland like Lystra and Derbe (Acts 13, 27). This premise places the epistle among Paul's earliest writings, possibly in 48 A.D. or even before that, but most likely after the council of Jerusalem 49 or 50 A.D.

PURPOSE OF THE EPISTLE TO THE GALATIANS

False Teachers of the Church

False teachers known as Judaizers (Jewish-Christian legalists) followed St. Paul in Galatia, opposing his doctrine concerning the disregard of the ceremonial law by Gentile converts, whilst also calling into question his apostolic authority (1:1-12). St. John Chrysostom says that some of the Jews who believed, being held down by the prepossession of Judaism at the same time, were intoxicated by vaingloriousness and desired obtaining for themselves the dignity of teachers, came to the Galatians and taught them that the observance of circumcision, Sabbaths and new-moons were necessary, and that Paul in abolishing these things was not to be obeyed. For they said that Peter, James and John, the chiefs of the apostles and the companions of Christ, forbade them not to. He was single, but they were many, and were also pillars of the Church. They accused him too of acting a part; saying that this very man who forbids circumcision observes the rite elsewhere and preaches one way to you and another way to others.

The chief argument was the fact that it was agreed the law of Moses was divinely instituted, to which Christ had said He came "not to abolish but to fulfill the Law" (Matt 5:17). They asserted that salvation was impossible without it, and for the Gentiles salvation is available only if they first become Jews. In other words, they loaded the believers with the burden of Judaism, adding to it the simple gospel of Christ. They made light of Paul's apostolic role, holding him to be less informed than the Twelve (1:11-24). They succeeded in disturbing and confusing the minds of the Galatians, who tended more and more to follow their teaching as a surer way of salvation. Christianity would consequently have become to them a mere sect of Judaism.

Munck had proposed that the disturbers were not actually Jews, but were Gentile converts whose zeal led them to think that Judaism was a necessary part of the gospel. Most commentators believe that one cannot be so precise about the disturbers. It seems altogether probable that they are connected with the Judaising movement mentioned in Acts 15.

MAIN THEMES AND STRUCURE OF THE EPISTLE TO THE GALATIANS

Special Features of the Epistle to the Galatians

This is a fervent epistle, written with vigour and feeling. St. Paul throws himself without reserve into the proclamation of the gospel, it has a power unique among his writings. Its chief importance is theological. In it, we are met with many of the heaviest themes of St. Paul's preaching: justification by faith working through love, the new life in Christ, the responsibilities of love, the meaning of the Cross, the law of Christ, the function of the Mosaic law, and walking in the Spirit.

The Fervent Epistle

In this epistle, we find St. Paul being very firm, for the situation was critical and serious, as many of the believers were turned from the simplicity of the gospel to Judaism as if it were necessary for salvation. St. John Chrystosm writes about this:

The introduction is filled with a vehement and lofty spirit, which applies not only to the introduction, but also to the whole epistle. For always to address one's disciples with mildness, even when they need severity is not the part of a teacher but it would be the part of a corrupter and enemy...Paul has varied his discourse according to the needs of his disciples, at one time sharp, at another, applying mild remedies. To the Corinthians he says, "What will you? Shall I come unto you with a rod, or in love, and in a spirit of meekness?" (1 Cor 6:21) but to the Galatians he says, "O foolish Galatians." (Gal 3:1)

St John Chrysostom

This epistle reveals the organisation and structure of the Church in St. Paul's days. Cephas (St. Peter), St. James the Lord's brother and St. John, are named as Jerusalem apostles (1:18-19; 2:9). We read here of a Church council (2:1-10), for discussing practical theological topics and organising the mission field along ethnic lines (2:9); and of a dispute between two apostles (2:11-14).

It provides certain valuable data about St Paul's own life and ministry, yet it is not part of St. Paul's purpose to convey autobiographical information as such. It is only in the course of his total argument that these facts emerge. Scholars used to divide Galatians into personal, doctrinal and practical aspects, but in fact, it has one purpose: achieving practical freedom in Christ, as the true meaning of the gospel for life.

The Concept of Freedom in Christ

This epistle presents our Lord as our Liberator and it explains Christian liberty. Our Lord presents Himself as our Liberator, saying, "If the Son sets you, you will indeed be free" (John 8:36).

It is reckless to say that Liberty is freedom from law. It is a revolt against God and His order, and thus our civilisation will lapse into barbarism. Liberty is actually freedom within law. For example, upon entering a free public park, we might first see signs such as, 'Don't walk on the grass', 'No dogs allowed', 'Don't pick the flowers' etc. These laws are set in place to preserve the free park. Likewise, the Christian is urged to abandon the Law, not in order to be free and led by his own spirit (as this leads to barbarism and order is needed for preservation), but to be led by the Holy Spirit being the source of life and the director of its course (5:25).

V.P. Furnish says, "To a few commandments it has seemed more plausible that Paul's problem is with two different groups: legalists on the one hand and libertinisms on the other. Thus, he is compelled to fight on two opposite fronts at once. This dilemma explains his own perplexity (2:40) and the apparent shift in emphasis from the dangers of legalism (chapters 1-4) to the dangers of libertinism (chapters 5-6)."

Contrasts within the Epistle

This epistle contains many interesting contrasts, which are specified in a few ways:

1.Grace and Law (2:21):

We cannot say, "grace versus the Law," for the word 'law' in this epistle is used to mean "the legal observances," i.e. observing the rituals of the Law in its literal way which spoils the simplicity of our faith, received by grace. Law shows us our need for grace, which means God's undeserved kindness to us, that satisfies our needs.

2.Faith and works of the Law (2:15-20):

Faith makes us receive the divine grace, while observing the works of the Law reveals our weakness. St. Paul emphasises that true faith cannot be separated from good works, meaning that the spiritual works which are the action of the Holy Spirit in the lives of believers. Truly this letter concentrates on faith as the source of our sanctification, but that "faith working through love" (5:6) cannot separate true faith from good works. As an example, the thief who was crucified alongside Christ was a person of true faith, as he also did better than many of the disciples. Witnessing in these circumstances is truly a good act of faith.

3.Fruits of the Spirit and works of the flesh (5:19-6:6)

The Spirit gives us daily victory over sin, while the flesh makes us prone to sin.

4.The cross and the world (6:14):

The cross means self-giving, while the love of the world means selfishness. Through the cross, we receive an inner glory that is in contrast to the vainglorious (glory of this temporal world).

5.Dwelling in sin and being delivered from sin (1:4):

This epistle focuses on man's gospel, versus the gospel of Christ (1:6-9; man-pleasure and God-pleasure (1:10)); trusting in man's reasoning and Christ's revelation (1:11; 2:14); condemnation and justification (3:6-16);

lost in Adam and new in Christ (3:19-22); servants-in bondage and free sons-heirs (4:1-7); old covenant and new covenant (4:10-31); advancing in grace and falling from grace (5:6); walking in the Spirit and living in the flesh (5:17, 18) etc.

NOT LIVING IN EXTREMES AS CHRISTIANS

The Christian life, according to this epistle does not know extremes. Liberty is realised by freedom from the bondage of the literal observance of the works of the law, but not outside the law of Christ. Christian life is personal, a close and hidden contact with God; the believer is called and chosen by God himself, without ignoring His Church life, or the communal life.

All believers are one in Christ, but there are those who are pillars of the Church. In this epistle, our Lord Jesus Christ is seen as our Liberator, who came to grant us freedom and power. He is called our sin-bearer (1:4), Redeemer (3:13; 4:5), a curse for sinners (3:13), the Seed (3:19; 4:4), and the Justifier (2:16; 3:24).

True Liberation through the Son

As the epistle concentrates on the grace of God that makes us free from the burden of the Mosaic Law, it reveals the work of the Holy Trinity in the life of the believer, granting him inner liberty. The Father is called "our Father, to whom be glory forever" (1:4). He loves us, His own children to be glorified with Him eternally. This is our liberty, that we imitate our Father, and attain a great heart to love our brothers in mankind that they may participate in our heavenly gloried, i.e. He grants a universal spiritual love for all men.

The Son is our Liberator who paid His precious blood to grant us freedom from many things, including sins (1:4), this present evil age

(1:10), the curse of the law (3:13), the bondage of the works of the law (4:19 and from being under guardians (4:1-6).

The Son grants us participation in His crucifixion i.e. self-giving, as our true liberty. He became a servant for our sake, in Him we desire to be slaves to God and men, by our own will.

The Holy Spirit is the Spirit of adoption and not that of bondage. He works in us to bring us to the Father in Christ as His free children. The apostle refers to Him in this epistle:

• He is promised (3:14)

• He is sent forth (4:6)

• He ministers (3:5)

• He is received by faith (3:2)

• He indwells (4:6)

• He begins a task (3:3)

• He leads (5:18)

• He overcomes the flesh (5:16-18)

• He bears fruit (5:22-24

• He gives patience (5:5)

• He gives assurance (6:8)

Some scholars call this epistle "Luther's book," because he relied on it in his writings and arguments against the prevailing theology of his day, and he used to call it "my book."

Introduction to
THE EPISTLE TO
THE EPHESIANS

INTRODUCTION AND HISTORY

Ephesus is a Greek word which means "desired." It is the capital of the Roman colony on the left side of the Cayster River, west of Asia Minor, about three miles from the sea. It is almost in the middle between the city of Smyrna from the left, Miletus from the south, and it is where all the commercial roads meet, especially the main road between Rome and the East. An industrial port was built there, which gave it some great importance in the Middle Ages.

It was known for its great temple, Artemis, which is a goddess representing a mother who has many breasts, likely of Hathian origin. To the Greeks, it is considered the moon goddess, like Diana to the Romans. It appears as a virgin, tall and beautiful, sister of Apollo. They believed that her statue descended from heaven, and often it is drawn in the shape of a fisherman.

The Ionians, who are of Greek origin, occupied the city of Ephesus in 11 B.C., and it became one of the twelve cities in their union and the capital of Ionia.

In the year 555 B.C., the city fell under the reign of Croesus, the King of Lydia, (its capital is Sardes). After a short while, it went under the

Persian rule. During the reign of Alexander the Great, it was under the Greek Macedonian rule. In the year 133 B.C., it came under the Roman rule and became the capital of Asia.

In the year 29 B.C., an earthquake demolished the city and Emperor Tiberius ordered its reconstruction.

AUDIENCE OF THE EPISTLE

Who was this Epistle sent to?

In some of the old Greek manuscripts, the word "Ephesus" was not mentioned at all. That is why some scholars thought that it was a periodical message written for all the churches in Asia Minor, especially the church of Laodicia, and that it was referred to as Ephesus because it was the capital of Asia Minor at that time.

In saying this, the scholars rejected the theory of it being a "periodical message", although every group has their own point of view and their proofs. The first group emphasises that this epistle was a general periodic message. Their proof was that St. Paul never mentioned special greetings to any of the ministers in Ephesus, although he had many memories there since he is the one who had established it. Also, there was no handling to any of the specific problems as the rest of the epistles. They also say that referring to the book of Revelation, (Rev. 3:16), where we find that the Lord Jesus who is risen from the dead, declares that the name Laodicia will be removed from His mouth. And truly, Laodicia was replaced by Ephesus. In the second century, Marcion started with an idea that this epistle was sent to Laodicia. Some of the church fathers objected saying that it was originally sent to Ephesus. Among the fathers who proclaimed that idea was Tertullian the scholar, St. Clement of Alexandria, St. Irenaeus, Origen, and St. Moratory.

The other group objecting to the theory of "the periodic message", believe that this epistle was recorded during the last days of St. Paul while he was in prison at Rome. They believe that St. Paul is directing it not to the church at Ephesus as a whole, but to the members who were of Gentile origin, to people whom he did not know, who had accepted the faith and baptism after his departure from that city. He knows the church of Ephesus which he had established, but here he talks to the Gentiles about the concept of "the universal church." He did not want to mention names to elevate them above the personal relationships. However, in the other epistles, he addresses certain local problems, so he emphasised individual relationships. These are two complimenting concepts, which are apparent in St. Paul's life. As a true shepherd, he wanted to know each one in the flock, on a personal level in Christ Jesus, but in the meantime, he wanted to lift his eyes above the events to see the church of Christ as one and universal, without being partial to any person.

Time and Place of Writing

St. Paul does not show when he wrote this epistle nor where, but he made it clear that he is the prisoner of the Lord Jesus. He said, "I, Paul, the prisoner of Christ Jesus for you Gentiles…" (Eph. 3:1) "I ask that you do not lose heart at my tribulation for you, which is your glory." (Eph. 3:13) "I, therefore, the prisoner of the Lord…" (Eph. 4:1) "For which I am an ambassador in chains…" (Eph. 6:20)

The correct opinion is that it was written in the year 63 A.D., when he was under house arrest in Rome for two years. He received all who came to him, preaching the kingdom of God and teaching the things which concern the Lord Jesus Christ (Acts 28:30). During those two years, he wrote the epistles of Colossians, Ephesians, Philippians, and Philemon.

Some researchers like Reuss and Mayer believe that St. Paul wrote the epistles to the Ephesians, to the Colossians, and to Philemon from his prison in Caesarea (Acts 23: 35 & 24:27), between the years of 58 A.D. and 60 A.D. Mayer presented four proofs to support this, which we refute as follows:

1. Onesimus could have gone to Caesarea and not have gone on this long trip to Rome:

We refute that by saying that it is more acceptable that Onesimus, the robber and slave, would have gone first to Rome because it is far from Philemon, his master, lest he find him and kill him. Secondly, Rome is vast, and he can hide there without anyone noticing where he was, not like Caesarea, a small city where anyone could find him easily.

2. If these epistles were written in Rome, Onesimus and Tychicus would have carried the epistles to Ephesus before reaching Colossi. It would have been natural that St. Paul refers to them in his epistle to the Ephesians, as he did in his epistle to the Colossians (4:9). However, never mentioning both of them in his epistle to the Ephesians was due to his coming from Caesarea to Colossi, where Onesimus settled there and did not go with Tychicus to Ephesus. That is why there was no need to mention the name Tychicus.

To refute that, we say that the epistle to the Ephesians was a periodic epistle to all the churches in Asia Minor, so there is no need to mention Onesimus too.

3. His saying, "But that you also may know my affairs and how I am doing..." (Eph. 6:21) refers to Tychicus crossing first to Colossi then to Ephesus. He did that by going from Caesarea and not through Rome.

To refute this, the word "also" has many interpretations here. It means that the epistle to the Colossians was first written and carried its news to the entire region. Then this epistle was written to continue the news that Tychicus will inform them with new matters also.

4. St. Paul asked that Philemon prepare a place for him (Phil. 1:22). This means that St. Paul was near Caesarea.

To refute that, St. Paul was not talking about hastily going to him. Church tradition confirms that the epistles of captivity were written from Rome and not from Caesarea, especially what was mentioned in Ephesians 6:19,20 clarifies that St. Paul had some freedom which he used to preach the Gospel, and it is the same in Rome. (Acts 28: 16), and not in Caesarea (Acts 24:23)

ESTABLISHING THE CHRISTIAN CHURCH IN EPHESUS

In Ephesus, there were many Jews with a Roman citizenship (Acts 18:19 & 19:17). At the end of St. Paul's second missionary trip (about 54 A.D.), on his return to Jerusalem, he visited Ephesus where he preached in their synagogue. There he left Aquila and Priscilla to continue his work (Acts 18: 18-21) and promised the Jews that he would return to them very soon.

During his absence, Apollos came from Alexandria, who was one of St. John the Baptist's disciples. He preached in the synagogue only about what he had known about the Lord Christ, but Aquila and Priscilla taught him the way of the Lord more accurately. (Acts 18: 24-26).

According to his promise, St. Paul returned in 54 A.D., or on his third missionary trip, where he found some disciples who had not accepted Christ entirely. They had only accepted the baptism of John the Baptist, so he preached to them about the Lord Jesus and baptised them. Putting his hand on them and the Holy Spirit descended on them and they started talking with different languages and prophecy (Acts 19: 3-9).

St. Paul preached in the synagogue of the Jews for three months. When the unbelieving Jews attacked him, he left them and preached in a school of Tyrannus for two years until all who dwelt in Asia heard the word of the Lord Jesus, both Jews and Greeks. (Acts 19: 8-12)

The results of St. Paul's preaching in Ephesus, as St. Luke wrote in the book of Acts were as follows:

1. Many of the Jews and Gentiles accepted the faith of the Lord Jesus. (Acts 19:10)

2. The word of God reached all over Asia, through its capital, Ephesus. (Acts 19:10)

3. Since God worked unusual miracles by the hands of Paul (Acts 19:11), some of the itinerant Jewish exorcists called the name of the Lord Jesus, whom Paul preaches, over those who had evil spirits (Acts 19: 13), while many of those who had practiced magic brought their

books together and burned them in the sight of all. They counted up the value of them and it totalled fifty thousand pieces of silver. (Acts 19:19)

4. The worship of Artemis was abolished, which made the craftsmen angry, causing them to riot, attacking the preaching of St. Paul and considering it an insult to the great temple. (Acts 19: 24-29)

5. The establishment of a great church in Ephesus, with many priests, was mentioned in Acts chapter 20. In Miletus, (south of Ephesus), after preaching in Macedonia and Achaia, St. Paul called all the priests of Ephesus and told them about the false prophets who are like savage wolves who do not spare the flock. (Acts 20:29)

When St. Paul left Ephesus, his disciple Timothy went to serve there so that they may teach no other doctrine (1 Tim. 1: 3). Tychicus was sent to Ephesus, with this epistle (Eph. 6: 21 & 2 Tim. 4:12). It is likely he gave some copies to other churches in Asia, as well as sending out a special epistle to the Colossians.

The church of Ephesus was one of the seven churches in Asia mentioned in the book of Revelation (Rev. 1:11 & 2: 1-7). According to church tradition, St. John spent his last days in Ephesus and later departed on the island of Patmos, which is across from Ephesus.

In the year 431 A.D., the third ecumenical council was held there to attack the heresy of Nestor, who was the patriarch of Constantinople, who said that the Lord Jesus had two natures, considering that the divinity came upon Him on His baptism.

Now, the saying that Ephesus left her first love has been fulfilled, and that He is about to move her lampstand (Rev. 2:4), for it was transformed to the village of "Ephis", where no Christians lived anymore.

THE FOUR PROOFS THAT THE EPISTLE WAS WRITTEN BY ST. PAUL

The First Proof - The Inner Witness

D. Guthrie attested that the fingerprints of St. Paul are so obvious in this epistle. For the divine inspiration works in the writer to guide him and keep him from erring, without losing his personality, honouring his individuality, which the Holy Spirit uses and interacts with.

St. Paul's personality is apparent in many ways throughout this epistle. It instils the spirit of hope in the souls of the believers, as well as encourages them, thanking God for the news of the one who writes to them, saying, "Therefore, I also, after I heard of your faith in the Lord Jesus and your love for all the saints, do not cease to give thanks for you, making mention of you in my prayers…" (Eph. 1:15,16).

He calls himself a "…prisoner of Christ Jesus…" (Eph. 3:1), "I, therefore, the prisoner of the Lord…" (Eph. 4:1). He writes as a prisoner, imprisoned on behalf of faith. He writes about the "mystery of Christ", declared to him personally, for he says, "how that by revelation He made known to me the mystery… of which I became a minister according to the gift of the grace of God given to me by the effective working of His power." (Eph. 3:3,7)

As usual, the apostle points his practical love to whom he writes, for he considers his afflictions for them, asking them not to be occupied with his afflictions but to look above to the eternal glory, considering his afflictions glory not for himself, but for them also, for he says, "Therefore, I ask that you do not lose heart at my tribulations for you, which is your glory." (Eph. 3:13). He practices his practical love toward all of the human race, not only through his preaching and enduring afflictions for them, but also through prayers and interceding for them, in the spirit of humility. "For this reason, I bow my knees to the Father of our Lord Jesus Christ… that He would grant you according to the riches of His glory to be strengthened with might through His Spirit

in the inner man, that Christ may dwell in your hearts through faith…"
(Eph. 3:14-21)

St. Paul was a preacher to the Gentiles, always calling them to the new life and the new thought, and forsaking the gentile life with its futile mind, "This I say, therefore, that you should no longer walk as the rest of the Gentiles walk, in the futility of their mind… be renewed in the spirit of your mind, and that you put on the new man which was created according to God, in true righteousness and holiness." (Eph. 4: 17-24

In the spirit of humility, he prays for them and for all the church, for he says, "Praying always with all prayer and supplication in the Spirit, being watchful to this end with all perseverance and supplication for all the saints and for me, that utterance may be given to me, that I may open my mouth boldly to make known the mystery of the gospel." (Eph. 6: 18,19). As usual, he concludes the epistle by the apostolic blessing. (Eph. 6: 23,24). His introduction corresponded to the introduction of his second epistle to the Corinthians and his epistle to the Colossians.

His fingerprints are very apparent in the general skeleton of this epistle, which is very unique of his character, for the epistle started with the introduction, thanksgiving, talking about the dogma, instilling good conduct, conclusion and the apostolic blessing.

The Second Proof - The Outer Proofs

In spite of the inner proofs showing that this epistle was written by St. Paul, there are also outer proofs which confirm that. This epistle had wide acceptance in the middle of the second century in the Orthodox Church, even amongst the heretics. St. Clement the Roman, St. Ignatius the bishop of Antioch, Polycarp the bishop of Smyrna, Hermas in his book "The Shepherd"7, the "Didache" which is the Lord's teachings to the twelve apostles, and the heretic Merkion, mentioned it among the canonical books (around year 140 A.D.) under the name of "The Epistle to the Laodicians." It was also mentioned under the Muratorian Canon around the year 180 A.D., among the epistles of St. Paul.

OBJECTIONS ABOUT THE WRITER
OF THE EPISTLE AND HOW TO REFUTE THEM

First Objection regarding the linguistic and stylistic arguments

Some scholars and critics like Goodspeed, object that the epistle contains many Greek words that were never used in any of St. Paul's other epistles, hapax legomena (36 words). Moreover, they were never used in the whole of the New Testament (42 words). St. Paul used to use the word "Satanas" (Satan), but here he uses the word "diabolos" (devil) (Eph. 4:27) (as well as in the pastoral epistles).

On the other hand, its style and language are close to the first epistle of St. Clement the Roman (in the era following St. Paul's), more so than to St. Paul's epistles. The scholars refute these objections by the following three points:

1. The different vocabulary goes back to the different nature, for this epistle is unique as a "liturgical epistle", which contained some of the liturgical praises seeing as its main topic is "the church." Some of the vocabulary was derived from the liturgical church. Some explain that the different vocabulary goes back to the one whom St. Paul was dictating to while in prison, for he used many writers.

2. This epistle is very related to the first epistle of St. Clement the Roman, because the latter derived a lot of its vocabulary from the first.

3. In spite of the fact that this type of epistle is liturgical, different than all the other epistles, it is still very close to St. Paul's writings. In its essence, it carries the type and fingerprints of St. Paul, which makes it very difficult to say that it is not his. It is very obvious that it is St. Paul's style of writing.

Second Objection - Literary Arguments

Some critics say that these objections are major. The most important one is the great similarity between this epistle and the epistle to the Colossians. More than a fourth of the words used in the epistle to the Ephesians were derived from the epistle to the Colossians, while more than a third of the words used in the epistle to the Colossians were repeated in the epistle to the Ephesians. (There are 83 words common in both epistles). Critics say that it is impossible for such a scholar with renewed thought like St. Paul, to repeat the same words in two epistles, especially when he sometimes uses the same word for two different meanings. The word "mystery" in the epistle to the Colossians refers to Christ, while in the epistle to the Ephesians it refers to the unity of the Jews with the Gentiles.

Goodspeed concluded that the epistle to the Ephesians was not written by St. Paul, but by someone else who adopted parts from St. Paul's letters, especially from the epistle to the Colossians.

We can refute the literary argument, however:

The epistle to the Ephesians, as some scholars perceive it, is a periodic epistle to all the churches of Asia Minor, especially the Laodiceans (Col. 4:16). The epistle to the Ephesians was recorded as the capital of Asia Minor. Laodicea and Colossi are two cities close to each other, which is why St. Paul asked to exchange the epistles (Col. 4:16). During this time in particular, they were written close to each other and were carried by the same person, "Tychicus" (Eph. 6:21 & Col. 4:7). Also, both epistles discussed two topics which compliment one another. The epistle to the Ephesians discussed the church as the body of Christ, while the epistle to the Colossians discussed the topic of "Christ the Head of the Church." That is why they are very similar. This similarity does not make us doubt that the writer is one, but on the contrary, confirms that. What the critics considered as an objecting proof is a proof against them.

If another writer had adopted words from St. Paul's epistles, he would have adopted complete expressions. However, we see that common words in the two epistles confirm that the epistle was written by St. Paul.

Using common words in the two epistles (Ephesians and Colossians) with two different meanings, does not mean that the epistle was not written by St. Paul. On the contrary, it confirms that it belongs to St. Paul, who thought widely enough that a word can provide more than one meaning to an expression. When he speaks to the Colossians about "Christ the Head of the church", he talks about the "mystery" being "the mystery of Christ." In the epistle to the Ephesians when he talks about "the church as the Body of Christ," he talks about the mystery as the union of the church with Christ, whether those of Gentile origin or Jewish origin. Although the two meanings are different, we find them complementing one another and not conflicting.

The Third Proof - Historical Arguments

Some critics state that there is a difference between these epistles and the rest of St. Paul's epistles from the historical aspect. In this epistle, we see that the conflict between the Jews and the Gentiles has settled, while in the other epistles, we see that the conflict is still very apparent. This is the reason why critics have considered that this epistle was written at a later era than the era of St. Paul.

To refute that, we mention the following:

When writing about the reconciliation between the Jews and the Gentiles through the cross in one body "Putting to death the enmity …" (Eph. 2:14-16), he wrote in a language which characterises St. Paul's writings, the minister of the Gentiles who concentrated his writings on "breaking down the middle wall of separation", before breaking down the walls of Jerusalem to be opened for everyone.

If the epistle were written after St. Paul's era, there would not have been silence regarding the fall of Jerusalem when the middle wall of separation between the Jews and Gentiles was broken…This confirms that it was written during St. Paul's era. Moreover, not mentioning the persecution implies that it was written at an earlier time, before the church history that is in the apostolic age.

The Fourth Proof - Doctrinal Arguments

Some critics denied the authorship of St. Paul because of the differences in doctrines mentioned here than in the other epistles, which pertain to "the church, Christ, social doctrines." We do not want to go into details regarding these doctrines, however, we clarify that there is no contradiction between what was mentioned here and what was mentioned in the other epistles. In saying this, there are differences which give the epistle vitality instead of repetition and reveal the depth of the divine thought of St. Paul, without rigidity. This epistle is unique in its topic, which is to reveal the "universality of the church" and its uniqueness in adopting the church liturgical praises.

Some of the differences, which the critics mentioned, are as follows:

Regarding the special teaching of the church, in the other epistles, St. Paul emphasised the local churches and was concerned about the practical and dogmatic problems, presenting special greetings to beloved ministers working in the Lord's vine. However, in this epistle, we do not find any of that, because the theme of the epistle is "the universality of the church" (Eph. 4:1-16). Talking about this matter, he elevates us above the conditions of the church of Ephesus, its events, its problems and those working in it to declare the oneness of the church, the Body of Christ and His bride (Eph. 2:8,9 & 4:14 & 5:6). This is the main theme of the epistle, all in harmony with the apostolic thought.

Talking about the apostles and the prophets, St. Paul presents them as saints (Eph. 3:5) and as a foundation for the church where Christ is the cornerstone (Eph. 2:20). Some believed that this thought, which carries great veneration to the apostles and the prophets, represents the era after the apostolic age where all the apostles have departed and where the church is honouring them. This conflict is not logical, however, as sometimes St. Paul called the believers saints (Rom. 1:7). His writing about the apostles and the prophets as foundation to the church is definitely St. Paul's thought. He recorded it here when mentioning the universal church.

Writing about marriage (Eph. 5:21-33) gives it a special holiness which correlates to the concept of the unity of the church with Christ. We do not find this in his mentioning of marriage in his epistle to the Corinthians (1 Cor. 7:1-9). The reason why this is the case, is that in the epistle he presents a general picture of the understanding of the sacrament of holy matrimony, whilst in First Corinthians chapter seven, he presents an answer to a specific question.

PURPOSE OF THE EPISTLE

The Aim of the Epistle

This epistle is considered the "church type" in its essence. Its main subject is "the church" and Christ's relationship with the church. To Christ, the church is the body in relation to the Head (Eph. 1:22-23) and the bride to the Bridegroom (Eph. 5: 23-32).

The purpose of the epistle is to declare God's plan to create messianic people, a holy congregation united with the Head, Jesus Christ. This is the secret of God's love to humanity.

After St. Paul has confirmed, in the first three chapters, that salvation is for the Jews as well as the Gentiles, he emphasised in the last three chapters that unity of faith, holiness, social behaviour, and the spiritual weapons for the believer are practiced through the church and within it. Many scholars call this the "Crown of Paulinism."

MAIN THEMES AND STRUCTURE OF THE SECOND EPISTLE TO THE CORINTHIANS

Special Features of the Epistle

This epistle has been characterised by its concern for the apostolic church thought. Hence, it carried special types and unique traits.

The Church in Song and Praise

This epistle represents a church song or praise, on which St. Paul meditates. He sees that the veil obstructing the Jews and Gentiles has been demolished and the cross has destroyed the enmity. Therefore, this epistle is liturgical and hymnodic, where St. Paul encourages everyone to talk with psalms and spiritual songs (Eph. 5: 19).

It also contained some praises which were used during his age. Some excerpts of these praises are seen in the following verses: Eph. 1:3 –14, 20 – 23 & 2: 4 – 7, 10, 14 – 18, 20 – 22 & 3: 5, 20-21 & 4: 4 – 6, 11 –13 & 5: 2, 14, 25 –27). All of these excerpts had affected the language of the epistle and its style.

The Unique Literary Style of the Epistle

Within this epistle, verbs exceeded the nouns; there were 231 verbs versus 158 nouns, while in Galatians, there were 139 verbs versus 202 nouns, and in Romans, there were 363 verbs versus 377 nouns. Many pronouns were used like "for, therefore, that…" These were used at the beginning of the sentence or at its end, and some expressions were used in the middle of sentences. Often, the name of God was not mentioned but he said, "through Him or by Him…" St. Paul also mentions those who benefited from God's blessings in the first person, in plural form. For example, "Our Father, our Lord, blessed us, chose us…"

The Church as the Bride of Christ

St. Paul mentions the church as the bride of Christ united with the Father through His Son. He demonstrates God as the God of glory (Eph. 1:17), God of might (Eph. 1:19), and God the merciful (Eph. 2:4). He talked about the church as "in Christ", for in Him we receive heavenly blessings (Eph. 1:3). In Him He has chosen us (Eph. 1:4), and in Him we have redemption (Eph. 1:7), etc. He declared the power of His cross in the reconciliation (Eph. 2) and demonstrated the work of the Holy Spirit (Eph. 2:18, 3:5, 4:1-3, 5:18). In other words, the church is the work of the love of the Father, the Lover of mankind, and the work of the Son who gathered her through the cross and the work of the Holy Spirit, the donor of fellowship.

The Heavenly Nature of the Church

Since St. Paul declared the universal church in her hidden union with her Heavenly Bridegroom, he emphasises her heavenly nature, lifting our hearts up to heaven. In the introduction, he says, "Blessed be the God and Father of our Lord Jesus Christ, who has blessed us with every spiritual blessing in the heavenly places in Christ" (Eph. 1:3). We can say that by "heavenly places", he means that the church life is like a small deposit of heaven!

When mentioning the work of the Father in Christ the Head of the church, he writes, "He raised Him from the dead and seated Him at His right hand in the heavenly places" (Eph. 1:20). Through Him, we rise from the death of sin and we sit in the heavenly places, that is, we practice the church life as "life in the Heavenly Christ." Then, he repeated, "And raised us up together and made us sit together in the heavenly places in Christ Jesus." (Eph. 2:6)

In the third chapter, he declares, "To the intent that now the manifold wisdom of God might be made known by the church to the principalities and powers in the heavenly places." (Eph. 3:10). Even our struggle against the devil is achieved for the sake of heaven. "For we do not wrestle against flesh and blood, but against the rulers of the darkness of this age, against spiritual hosts of wickedness in the heavenly places." (Eph. 6:12)

Hence, we see the heavenly path very clearly, for the church is a heavenly life, and our Father is Heavenly and our Christ sits at the right hand in the heavens, and the enemy fights us every day to deprive us of heaven.

The Holiness of the Church

This epistle had demonstrated the holiness of the church as life with Christ, a heavenly life yet factual and liveable. St. John Chrysostom said in his sermon about the fall of Etrobios, "Nothing is settled like the church, she is your salvation and refuge! She is above the heavens and close to the earth; she does not get old. Many names cannot describe her, for she is the bride, the daughter, the virgin, the mother, and also the queen."

Christ the Glorified, not the Sufferer

Many researchers noticed that this epistle emphasised the glorified Lord Jesus, not the suffering Christ, for this is the epistle of the hidden church. Although she participated in the suffering of Christ, she hopes to enjoy the fellowship of His heavenly glories. This is the epistle of the Lord of glory, the glorified Father and the glorified Son. That is why in the first chapter, we find the words "the praise of His glory" repeated three times (Eph. 1:6,12,14). By practicing the church life, we present the song of "the praise of His glory", not only by our lips but also by all our life.

The Epistle and its Gnostic Approaches

Since 1835, F. C. Baur believed that this epistle carried Gnostic approaches, which appeared in the second half of the second century. The researchers were concerned about the relation of this epistle to the Gnostic writings, especially after the famous Nagah Hamadi Gnostic reprints. Some thought that this epistle had some Gnostic thoughts and at the same time, anti-Gnostic ones. The reason for that is that he used their expressions but in a completely different understanding, which we have aforementioned. For example, St. Paul often mentioned the word "knowledge", but he does not present "gnosis knowledge", according to the Gnostic thought, which means that the mind replaces the faith. However, he mentions knowledge as a heavenly gift declaring what is hidden and that its purpose is salvation, which attaches to the one who obtains it from God on the road of a spiritual life, whose centre is the Lord Christ.

Introduction to
THE EPISTLE TO
THE PHILIPPIANS

INTRODUCTION AND HISTORY

This epistle is considered the sweetest of the epistles written by the apostle Paul. It is as though it is an essay sent by him to the Church in all eras and to every believer during all times. It encourages them, exhorting them to live perpetually exulting in spite of any situation prevailing around them through practicing the new life that knows no idleness, but is an unceasing motion through Jesus Christ.

The apostle wrote this epistle to a congregation with which he had a special relationship of love with. Due to their relationship, they provided him with gifts to spend on the message of the Gospel; whether that concerns his necessary needs, or those of the ministers accompanying him, even after his departure from among them to Corinth or to Thessalonica.

While in his first imprisonment in Rome, although the apostles were put under house arrest and guarded by Roman soldiers for the duration of two years, he was banned from travelling to other countries or cities, or even from going to other houses within the same city to preach the gospel. Yet, as he hesitated, his chains led to more progress in his ministry. They were not able to keep him from testifying the gospel nor make him lose the exulting life he had in Christ Jesus:

The apostle Paul found in his prison a chance to talk to the Roman guards and officials about our Lord Jesus, a unique chance to preach, which he could not let go. Realising that he was imprisoned for the sake of the Lord Christ and His gospel, the guards became interested in knowing more about both, which led some of them to believe.

The word of God is so strong and capable to transform the hosts of evil in this world of darkness, to confess the greatness of God, and to reveal His exalted work. We see how this happened when God used the Pharaoh of Egypt during the Exodus of the children of Israel; Herod, at the time of birth of the Lord Christ; those who mocked and scoffed the Lord during His crucifixion, and the guards at His tomb. The imprisonment provided the apostle Paul with the chance to write to the people beloved by him about the perpetual life exulted in the Lord.

Contrary to those who preached with envy and ulterior motives, there were others who preached with faithfulness, love and holy will. The apostle's friends, disciples and a multitude of believers became stronger in faith and more daring in preaching without fear, to partake of the apostle's honour as a captive of the Lord Christ.

His enemies worked hard to draw many heathens to faith with the purpose of stirring up the emperor and the rulers against Paul to keep them from setting him free. Some others used the imprisonment of the apostle Paul to appear as though they were more diligent in preaching the gospel, with the assumption that by doing so, they would belittle his status. In any case, even those who preached out of envy in order to add more sorrow to the apostle, on the contrary made him more exulted for the sake of the growth of the ministry of Lord Christ and the gospel (1:16-18).

History of Philippi

The name 'Philippi' means "a lover of horses or of war." It was considered the most important city in the whole region, on account that it is the first city reached by a sea traveler to Macedonia.

Originally known as 'Krenides', meaning "wells or springs", it was given the name 'Philippi' after King Philip the second of Macedonia, father of Alexander the Great. But after the Romans took over, it became a part of Macedonia.

Philippi is located north-east of Macedonia, north of Greece, nine miles away from the Aegean Sea. It sits on a prominent little hill surrounded by a fertile valley that made it an agricultural province, besides having mines of gold and silver nearby.

In the year 357 B.C., King Philip the second of Macedonia took over the province of 'Krenides' up the River of Nestos,' annexed it in his kingdom and made the city larger by adding more land to it, making it stronger to face any attack by enemies. Yet, it eventually fell under the authority of the Romans, becoming a Roman colony instead. When Octavius became emperor of the Roman empire and changed his name to 'Augustus Caesar,' he gave special care to the city of Philippi. He renewed it, made it even larger, and granted it the 'colonial status,' namely, a free Roman colony, whose inhabitants had the same rights and privileges enjoyed by the inhabitants of Rome, the capital. It started to develop more of a Roman culture than a Greek one, and it adopted the Latin language as its official language. The prevailing religion at the time was idol worship.

Authenticity of the Epistle

It is established that this epistle is written by the apostle Paul, as confirmed by all the early testimonials like those of Saints Polycarp, Erinaos, Cyprian, the scholar Origen, and others. Moreover, the style, teachings, and principles, all conform to the same in the other epistles written by the apostle Paul.

Further information about
the Church of Philippi

1. Because of the small number of Jews in Philippi, bigotry was less experienced there than it was in other cities.

2. This church had a special place in Paul's heart, because he went there according to a heavenly vision.

3. Feeling a great love for the apostle Paul, the Philippians sent him material support on more than one occasion.

4. It was a suffering church scoffed by adversaries, on account of that they worshipped someone condemned to death.

5. This church represented the home where Paul found comfort.

AUDIENCE OF THE EPISTLE

Preaching in Philippi

In the year 50 or 51 A.D., "a vision appeared to the apostle Paul in the night; a man of Macedonia stood and pleaded with him, saying: 'Come over to Macedonia and help us.' Now after he had seen the vision, he immediately sought to go to Macedonia, concluding that the Lord had called him to preach the gospel to them" (Acts 16:9,10). Accompanied by Silas, Luke the evangelist, and Timothy, they went to Philippi, the foremost city in the province of Macedonia. It was there that Paul took notice of the following points:

1. Paul was a Jew, while the Philippians were Gentile

2. Paul was proud of his Jewish origin, while the Philippians were proud of being Romans, although Paul himself had the Roman citizenship

3. Paul was Asian, while the Philippians were Europeans

4. Paul's mother tongue was Hebrew and he mastered the Greek language, while the Philippians spoke both Latin and Greek.

5. Paul's heart radiated the faith in Christ, while the Philippians lived in heathen abominations.

The apostle Paul visited 'Philippi' (Acts 16:11-40) during his second preaching trip, and there he established the first Christian Church in Europe. Once he arrived there, accompanied by Silas, Luke and Timothy, they went to the suburbs of the city on the riverside of the River 'Gengets,' (where the Jews used to pray every Sabbath day) and spoke to the women about salvation. Now a certain woman named Lydia, a rich seller of purple, heard the testimony of the apostles. The Lord opened her heart to faith, and she, together with her household, were baptised. She begged the apostle and his company to come and stay in her house. She became the first Christian in all of Europe, and Philippi became the first city in Europe to believe in the Christian faith (See Acts 16: 12, 15, 40).

St. Luke the Evangelist in the Book of Acts (16: 16-40), wrote about how an evil spirit of divination was driven out of a certain slave girl, who brought her masters much profit by fortune-telling. That girl followed Paul and his company, crying out and saying, "These men are the servants of the Most High God, who proclaim to us the way of salvation." Doing that for many days, Paul, greatly annoyed, turned and said to the evil spirit, "I command you in the name of Jesus Christ to come out of her," to which he instantly did (Acts 16: 16-18). Yet, our teacher Paul did not accept that testimony from the devil, the enemy of the Truth; because if he did, all the people present would have accepted all her words. But when her masters saw that their hope of profit was gone, they seized Paul and Silas, dragged them, and brought them to the magistrates saying, "These men, being Jews, exceedingly trouble our city, and they teach customs which are not lawful for us, being Romans, to receive or to observe." The magistrates tore all their clothes and commanded them to be beaten with rods. In this incident, we should notice the following:

1. The charge against them is not new; the devil used it on the tongues of the Jews against the Lord Christ Himself.

2. God, who allows evil and anguish to dwell upon His children, turns evil to good and anguish into comfort, through which His believers could see His wonders and experience His love and work in them.

3. Having their clothes torn, Paul and Silas rejoiced, because they had seen before their eyes Jesus Christ bearing Himself on the cross to cover our nakedness.

4. That sacrifice done by the two apostles represents the cross of preaching, the cost of the distribution of the gospel, and the salvation of souls from the hold of the devil.

5. It was an opportunity for 'Saul of Tarsus' to remember what he had previously done to the innocent Christians in persecution, beating, murder, and imprisonment… "I will show him how many things he must suffer for My name's sake" (Acts 9: 16).

Despite their suffering of imprisonment, injustice, and persecution, Paul and Silas at midnight were praying and singing hymns to God, and the prisoners were listening to them. Suddenly, there was a great earthquake, so that the foundations of the prison were shaken. Immediately, all the doors were opened, and everyone's chains were loosened. But Paul and Silas did not escape. Such an earthquake and other later wonders, like the movement of the Mokattam mountain near Cairo, reveal the limitless strength of the Christian faith that surpasses time, never becoming old.

The keeper of the prison, awakening from sleep and seeing the prison doors open, assuming that the prisoners had fled, drew his sword and was about to kill himself. But Paul called out with a loud voice, saying, 'Do yourself no harm for we are all here.' At that the prison keeper fell down trembling before Paul and Silas. They spoke the word of the Lord to him and to his household, who all received the Christian faith. The next day, when the magistrates heard that Paul and Silas were Roman citizens, they were embarrassed because they had beaten and imprisoned them without trial.

In short, the apostle Paul afterwards visited Philippi twice during his third preaching trip in about the years 57 and 58 A.D. (Acts 20: 1, 6). Later, when the Philippians heard about his imprisonment in Rome in the years 61-62 A.D, they sent Epaphroditus to him with a gift (4:

10) and directed him to stay and serve St. Paul. The Philippians were immensely distressed to hear that Epaphroditus fell sick almost unto death, and when he got well, Paul sent him back to the Philippians to rejoice, as they were longing to see him.

Time and Place of Writing

This epistle, together with those to the Ephesians, the Colossians, and to Philemon, were known as the 'captivity epistles', written while Paul was in his first captivity, or in prison in Rome (61-63). This epistle was the last of them, and Paul sent it with Epaphroditus

PURPOSE OF THE EPISTLE TO THE PHILIPPIANS

The Aim of the Epistle

The goal of writing this epistle as proclaimed by the divine inspiration, was to support the children of God before the afflictions of this world. It demonstrates a portrait of the believer as a saint, who, despite suffering bitter situations, is always rejoicing in the Lord. It shows us that the world cannot deprive us of the comfort in Jesus Christ, nor of experiencing the spiritual victory over all the disturbing circumstances. This epistle, indeed, shows us how our behavior in this world, our relationships with one another and with the others should be. We can summarise its purposes into six main ideas:

1. The Philippians worried about their beloved prisoner in Rome

2. They worried about preaching the gospel by the apostle to the Gentiles

3. This epistle was a call to rejoice in all circumstances; a call to fellowship in preaching the gospel (1: 5), in the grace of Christ (1: 7), in the Spirit of Christ (2: 1), in the passions of Christ (3: 10), in the afflictions for Christ's sake (4: 14), and in giving (4: 15)

4. He wrote to thank them for their generosity in giving

5. He wrote to counsel them and to warn them against the false teachers

6. There were no problems or dissensions worth mentioning; except some non-conformity between two female ministers in the church: 'Eudia' and 'Cyntyche', who caused some concerns in the apostle

MAIN THEMES AND STRUCTURE OF THE EPISTLE TO THE PHILIPPIANS

Special Features of the Epistle to the Philippians

There are no doctrine debates in this epistle; for the apostle's mind was wholly absorbed in the heavenly joy. What is proclaimed in this epistle is the active (dynamic) heavenly life, exulted in our Lord Jesus Christ; as shown in the fellowship in the Lord (4:1). Joy is the main feature in the relationship of the apostle with the church congregation. It supports the believers in enduring suffering and confronts the possibility of martyrdom.

To die with Christ is to Gain

We practice this joyful life here on this earth, as long as Christ is our life; and for us, to die is gain--it is a profit (1: 21). As well as this, we shall behold Christ face to face at our departure from this world, "Our desire is to depart and be with Christ, which is far better" (1: 23). We strive toward "the prize of the upward call of God in Christ Jesus" (3: 14).

Although "our citizenship is in heaven" (3: 20), St. Paul was not preoccupied with receiving the prize after death, but with preaching the gospel and turning his whole life into a glorification of the Lord Christ. If by his death he could glorify Christ, it would be "gain'; as long as the goal of his whole life is to glorify Christ.

Unity in the Holy Body

We anticipate Jesus Christ who will change our weak bodies to the likeness of His glorified body. We honor our bodies, because they will partake of the glories of our souls.

The apostle Paul counts the joy and crown of his people as his own (4: 1). The good minister practices the life of fellowship with those he ministers. He rejoices together with them and suffers when they confront troubles. And according to the words of the apostle Paul, he counts himself "labor in birth for them until Christ is formed in them" (Galatians 4: 19); and in the world to come, he will find them his crown.

The Joyful Epistle

He counts his ministry as a call for joy, "Rejoice in the Lord always. Again I will say, rejoice" 4:1).

"He counts all things as rubbish, that he may gain Christ" (3: 8), being our sufficiency and our treasure.

The apostle repeats the expression: "the day of Jesus Christ" (1: 6, 10); as a joyful day.

The apostle Paul refers to the meaning of the incarnation and salvation (2: 6-11).

The apostle proclaims his trust in the work of God: "I trust in the Lord that I myself shall also come shortly" (2: 24). He has confidence that the Lord will set him free of prison and bring him back to them.

The apostle trusted that God would work in the rulers of that country who were extremely evil and corrupted.

Through sanctifying our emotions, the apostle Paul not only lifts us up to see our bodies glorified and be in the likeness of the body of Jesus Christ risen from the dead, but he indirectly exhorts us not to destroy or repress our emotions, but to enjoy sanctifying them, saying, "I have you in my heart" (1: 7). "How greatly I long for you all with the affection of Jesus Christ" (1: 8). "Since he (Epaphroditus) was longing for you all, and was distressed because you had heard that he was sick. For indeed he was sick almost unto death" (2: 26, 27). "Therefore, if there is any … comfort of love, … if any affection and mercy, fulfill my joy by being like-minded, having the same love being of one accord, of one mind" (2: 1, 2).

Divine Grace and the Will of Man

The cooperation between the divine grace and the will of man is God's pleasure, that He may work through us by strengthening and sanctifying our will, should we choose to submit to Him. He wishes for us to be positive toward our salvation, "Work out your own salvation with fear and trembling; for it is God who works in you, both to will and to do for His good pleasure" (2: 12-13). The apostle Paul also wishes for us not to cease striving: "for the prize for the upward call of God in Christ Jesus" (3: 14).

Joy through Suffering

The apostle Paul not only diligently practiced the joyful life in the Lord, but he also became the source of joy for those suffering, being "poured out as a drink offering on the sacrifice and service of their faith" (2: 17-18). In the book of Exodus 29: 40, the drink offering refers to the joy through the suffering. Wine, as a symbol of the spiritual joy, is poured on the sacrifice (the suffering), to turn it into an inner joy.

The apostle Paul refers to the importance of 'delivery' (4: 6); which we sometimes call 'tradition.'

Life Through Christ

Because of the positive role of the congregation (the laic), St. Paul called them 'saints' and even referred this name to them before the bishops and deacons (1:1). Since the main topic of this epistle is life in Christ, reactive (dynamic) and exulting, the heavenly holy life, it is why St. Paul directed this epistle to the church as a whole, particularly to the congregation, who are called to be saints. It is also through the commitment of the bishops and the deacons, as they try to do their best to minister to the children of God, that help the congregation become saints.

The apostle Paul lived his life interceding for others. Even while in prison he used to pray for his friends, saying, "I thank God for every remembrance of you, always in every prayer of mine making request for you all with joy" (1: 3-4).

Introduction to
THE EPISTLE TO
THE COLOSSIANS

INTRODUCTION AND HISTORY

The city of Colossae was a small city in the district of Phrygian west of Asia Minor, east of Ephesus, west of Antioch and in Pisidia on the Lycos river. Lycos Valley was exposed to several earthquakes. As a result, precipitation from the Cretaceous period was exposed and toppled many of the district's landmarks.

Colossae is neighbouring two important cities: Laodicea and Hierapolis. The three of which were famous for the trade of wood and dyes. Due to the many volcanoes, the district became filled with pastures. This led to the prosperity of wool manufacturing and dyeing, which became a well-known product in Colossae, known as Colossian wool.

We do not know much of Colossae's history. Herodotus mentions that it was a great city in Phrygia and was very wealthy. However, it diminished over time, eventually becoming a small village by the time it was the era of St. Paul. Nothing is left in it at this point, other than the villages Chinos and Kinas, in Turkey. It is situated under the shadow of Mount Cadmiums, which is surrounded by high trees.

Within the suburban regions, we found in the suburbs of the old city of Colossae, the domes, arcs, and cobblestones. It was through these that we found connections between Colossae, Laodicea and Hierapolis because they were close in distance. Therefore, the apostle recommended that the epistle to the Colossians should be read in Laodicea and likewise, the epistle to Laodicea should be read in Colossae (1 Col. 4:16). Yosifious mentions that the Jews had lived in Phrygia for two centuries and that they had adopted the customs of the Gentile citizens there. Even the assimilated Jews who later accepted the Christian faith, brought with them the unique traits and customs of these Gentiles into the faith. Yusabius also mentions that Philip the deacon and his four virgin daughters lived in this region, and that their tombs were discovered in Hierapolis during the latter end of the second century.

AUDIENCE OF THE EPISTLE

The Service of Epaphras in Colossae

Upon the return of St. Paul from Ephesus, Timothy and Silas from the council of Jerusalem (Acts 15:9) preached within the regions of Phrygia and Galatia. After this, St. Paul travelled between the two of them in order to strengthen the disciples. Some think that St. Paul did not actually go to Colossae himself due to his recorded travels being along the northern regions (Acts 19:1), whereas Colossae is located in the southern region. It is for this reason that most scholars suggest it was likely Epaphras who preached in Colossae. Epaphras is referred to by St. Paul as, "Our dear fellow servant who is a faithful minister of Christ on your behalf" (1 Col. 1:7), as well as "Epaphras who is one of you" (4: 12), which supports the belief that he was someone who lived within Colossae. It is believed that Epaphras likely met St. Paul during his two-year stay in Ephesus, when he first accepted the faith through the apostle (Acts 19:10). However, some scholars believe that there is no significant evidence to support the belief that St. Paul did not actually preach in this region. They support this through the position that some of the Colossians accepted the faith through St. Paul's ministry while in Ephesus in 53-56 A.D.).

Time and Place of Writing

The epistle to the Colossians was written while in prison, just like the epistles to the Ephesians, Philippians and Philemon. In the early Church traditions, it states that the epistle was written in Rome during his first imprisonment there (Acts 28) between the years 61-63A.D. A number of scholars suggest that the epistles may have been written during his imprisonment in Caesarea (58-60 A.D) or Ephesus (55-56 A.D), however, it was most likely written in Rome, for the following reasons:

1. When St. Paul enumerated his co-ministers, he could not omit the evangelist Philip, with whom he had stayed with shortly before his imprisonment (Acts 21:8-14)

2. There is no mention in the Book of Acts of the widespread ministry that is written in the accompanying epistles of Ephesians and Philippians.

3. It is difficult to think that the runaway pagan slave, Onesimus, went to Cesarea, when it makes more sense that he would have gone to Rome, a place that was filled with others in similar circumstances.

4. St. Paul hoped for an early release (Philippians 1:19-25), however, this was out of the question because it is only by bribery that this could occur in Cesarea, which St. Paul would not have allowed for. However, we can expect that he could be released in Rome, likely during the second of the two years he was here, mentioned in Acts 28:30.

AUTHOR OF THE EPISTLE

There are external and internal pieces of evidence that support the idea that St. Paul is the writer of this epistle, which can be seen in the following points:

1. In the introduction, it was written that the authors were St. Paul and Timothy

2. Since St. Paul is the author of the epistle to Philemon, as he openly declared, " I am Paul writing with my own hand" (Philemon 1:19), we can compare some common points between the two epistles. An example of this is the mentioning of the names of the co-preachers who worked with the apostle, including Epaphras, Marstrchs, Dimas, and Luke. Similarly, the epistle to Philemon was written by Onsemious, while Onesimous delivered it with Tychicus to Colossae (Cols 4: 18). Both letters were written in his imprisonment in Rome (Cols 4: 1 1-24).

3. It is good to point out that the epistle has the same features as St. Paul's other epistles in its structure, where the introduction starts with giving thanks to God, then discusses the doctrine, followed by practical, daily ethics.

Objections to the Author of the Epistle

Some object that the style of this epistle is different from his style in the others. The answer to this is that the epistle has addressed a heresy that appeared in Colossae which required the apostle's writing about the dominion of our Lord Jesus over every creation and the nature of Christ and His wor. The epistle became a very important reference for our Church fathers, who relied on it to refute some heresies, particularly to disprove the Aryosan heresies.

Some also object that the epistle addresses the Gnosian inclinations, although Gnosticism did not attack Christianity, other than in the second century. As such, the author of the epistle must be after the first century. In reply to this, the Gnosians as separate entities, have claimed that they are Christians in the second century. However, it has tried to instil their ideologies in the Church through the Jews and the Helenians, who already had these inclinations. Gnosticism did not comprise separate groups under the leadership of a specific person, such as Marcion, Phlantions and Pasilide, other than in the second century, although it existed before Christianity where Jews and Helenians adopted it.

The teaching concerning the Lord Christ exceeds what came in the other epistles of St. Paul, particularly His role in creation, which proves that it was written after the apostolic era. The refute to this is that the eternal existence of Jesus Christ was also in the epistle to the Philippians (Phil. 2: 9-11). His role in creation was also referred to in (1 Cor 6: 8), and nobody doubted the authenticity of that sentence, which was written in the first epistle to the Corinthians.

Due to the great resemblance between these two epistles and to the one to the Ephesians, some scholars claim that it has depended on the latter epistle. We can refute this by comparing similar verses across both epistles. We learn that the verses in Colossians are older than the ones in Ephesians. There are also similar verses here to that in the epistle to the Philippians, which carry the same fervent and spiritual atmosphere.

THE PURPOSE OF THE EPISTLE TO THE COLOSSIANS

The Aim of the Epistle

The purpose of the epistle is observed from the sequence of the epistle itself. Epaphras went to Rome to deliver the good news about the Church in Colossae to St. Paul, where faith and love reigned (1: 4, 2:5). However, a heresy crept into the Colossian society which belittles the importance of Christ Jesus in a way that removes Him from his throne and denies His leadership to the Church. St. Paul sent this Epistle with Epaphras to fix this problem, but Epaphras was arrested and jailed, so the Apostle sent it with Tychicus.

Some note that the places surrounding Colossae suffered a lot because of the heresies, and the Apostle wanted to protect them against the heresies that were creeping up. He praises for the purposes of encouraging them, telling to be steadfast in faith and to refuse the strange heresies: "For though I am absent in the flesh, yet I am with you in spirit, rejoicing to see your good order and the steadfastness of your faith in Christ. As you therefore have received Christ Jesus the Lord, so walk in Him." (Co. 2: 5-6). While he wrote to the Galatians, "I marvel that you are turning away so soon from Him who called you in the grace of Christ, to a different gospel", "O foolish Galatians! Who has bewitched you that you should not obey the truth" (Gal. 1: 6, 3: 1).

Paul the Apostle concentrated this Epistle on our Master Christ, which is why he repeatedly mentions the Name of Christ in it. He also about the Sublimity and Divinity of the Lord Christ, assuring that He is God, One with the Father and equal to Him, excelling above all the other creatures, as if he was proclaiming, 'Do not allow anything to steal the place of Christ, and do not allow anyone to push you to deny Him.'

A Gnostic Jewish heresy and its Remedy

Historically, it seems that a group of Jews went to Phrygia and settled there. These groups accepted some Hellenic philosophies related to the Gnosticises, which they mixed with some Jewish traditions. They claimed that what they had gained from our Lord Jesus was not enough to fill their spiritual and behavioural needs, and that they were in need to immunise themselves against the unseen powers (whether they were the good or evil angels), including the worship that doctrine offered them.

The significant points of these incorrect principles

These heresies appeared into two fields: the field of ethical behaviour, and the field of doctrine and theology, where they wrongly affected the Lord Christ.

1. Some Jews accepted some Gnostic thoughts and combined them with Jewish thoughts. However, now that they also believed in Jesus Christ, they unfortunately brought to their faith the fingerprints of Gnostic and Jewish thought. Gnosis concentrated on knowledge, with 'Gnosis' being thought of as the way to connect with God. For them, knowledge is not a Divine gift granted to the believer through the Divine grace and His announcements, it is instead an enlightenment which a person enjoys during his personal struggle through asceticism and austerity.

Knowledge according to the Gnosticises is different than the Hellenists knowledge, although both deny that a person enjoys knowledge or wisdom as a Divine gift. The Gnostics see it as the struggle of a person through his asceticism, while the Hellenists see it as the struggle of a person through using his mind.

The Gnostics also believed that a person is connected to evil matter, and would never be able to come closer to God except through the angelic creatures, which help him towards redemption of the materialistic world and sin. At the same time, some Hellenist philosophers consider that there are many Aeons that are able to lift the person above the materialistic world, taking him gradually to the Greatest Being. It is likely that the number of these Aeons was 12, each sending the person to an Aeon higher than it in spirituality.

2. Worshipping the angels was also of significant incorrect principle. The Apostle wrote to them, "Let no one cheat you of your reward, taking delight in false humility and worship of angels, intruding into those things which he has not seen, vainly puffed up by his fleshly mind" (Col. 2: 18).

They also misused the explanation of the verse, "Then God said, "Let Us make man in Our image," {Gen. 1: 26}, claiming that God made the angels create the human being. They reached a stage of belief whereby the Lord Christ Himself was subdued to their authority, especially when He came down to earth and His Ascension after His Resurrection to Heaven. That is why the Epistle assures that our Lord Christ is The Creator of the heavenlies, as He is always The Creator of earth and the entirety of humanity (Col. 2: 15).

3. In order to please these angels, they had to refrain from eating and drinking certain kinds of foods and drinks because they are defiled, and they should practice literal duties: do not touch, do not taste, do not feel. They claimed that asceticism satisfies a person's spiritual needs and fulfils his reconciliation with God. The Apostle assured that the literal practices could never renew the human nature which was spoiled by sin. Instead, renewal is achieved through the burial with Christ in the Baptism, where we are graced with the resurrected life as well (Col. 2: 12). Thus, the struggle becomes legal and fruitful, "since you have put off the old man with his deeds and have put on the new man who

is renewed in knowledge according to the image of Him who created him" (Col.3: 10).

4. They considered the materialistic creation as rotten and defiled, including the human body, and that is why they refused the incarnation of Christ--that He became a true Man with a true Body. They also claimed that there are different ranks for the angels, and that among them, there are some who can mediate to God for a person without Christ.

5. Some thought that the Lord Christ was one of the intercessors, a Saviour among the Saviours and an intercessor among other intercessors. The Epistle revealed Christ's atoning intercession based on the Sacrifice of the Cross {Col. 1: 14}, and His intercession was accepted, so we had life with Him with the forgiveness of all our sins (Col. 2: 12-13). The Apostle revealed that what the Gnosticises were calling for was just arrogance according to the people's tradition (Col.2: 8, 18).

6. Those Jews could not get rid of their Jewish background, thus they thought that salvation was achieved by literally practicing the rituals, formalities and the Mosaic Commandments, such as the tradition of keeping the Sabbath, monthly and annual feasts, refraining from unclean foods, practicing circumcision...etc. They used to come closer to God through the angels, and they continued doing Jewish and Greek practices. The Apostle amended these issues.

It is worth mentioning that the Gnosticism's effects and the Judaism movement had spread to other Churches such as the Corinthians, which was reflected in denying the resurrection of the body, allowing adultery, underestimating the body, and misunderstanding asceticism...etc.

Gnosticism was not connected to Christianity straightaway, however, it clung to some of the scattered Jews.

The Gnostic direction of thought was a religious and philosophical way of thinking, more than a definite regime, which was able to attract atheists, Jews, and then Christians. In the second century, the

Gnostic movements appeared and then became groups which formed dangerous leaders who had influence over many. These Gnostic groups were different from each other, but there were a few general things they had in common. I had addressed the Gnosticises in detail in our study of The School of Alexandria.

MAIN THEMES AND STRUCTURE OF THE EPISTLE TO THE COLOSSIANS

Similarities Between the Epistle to the Colossians and the Epistle to the Ephesians

The owner of the Epistle to the Colossians, the Epistle to the Ephesians and the Epistle to Philemon, wrote them all at the same time. He wrote the Epistle to the Ephesians which was delivered by Tychicus, the Epistle to Philemon delivered by Onesimus, and to the Colossians delivered by both Tychicus and Onesimus.

The two Epistles are similar because they were addressed to two close districts in Asia Minor, the citizens of both districts had common social and behavioural traits, and both populations did not have Jewish origins, but they were Gentiles. In both Epistles, St. Paul revealed the secret of God's plan in accepting the Gentiles and for sharing the Jews in the Heavenly Inheritance, as the Lord Christ had abolished the enmity and created in Himself one new man from two (Eph. 2: 15), "the mystery which has been hidden from ages and from generations, but now has been revealed to His saints. To them God willed to make known what are the riches of the glory of this mystery among the Gentiles" (Col. 1: 26, 27).

Although the two Epistles are similar in wording, each one of them focuses on a certain aspect. The Epistle to the Ephesians talked about all the believers as the one body for Christ, but the Epistle to the Colossians concentrated on One Head for the Body: Jesus Christ.

The first talked about the Church of Christ, and the second about The Christ of the Church, and both are integral.

Some scholars consider the Epistle to the Ephesians as a natural extension to the Epistle to the Colossians. The latter highlighted the status of the Lord Christ and His work to refute the Gnostic thought which underestimated the status of The Master and withheld His level. The Epistle to the Ephesians came to presenting the outcome of the work of Master Christ, i.e. the Church, the Body of Christ which was in the plan of God before the establishment of the world, and that it is the most beloved bride for him, through which "to the intent that now the manifold wisdom of God might be made known by the church to the principalities and powers in the heavenly places" (Eph. 3: 11).

Main Ideas of the Epistle

1. The Person of Jesus Christ:

The Gnostic perspectives attacked the personality of Jesus Christ, which is why St. Paul concentrated here on the greatness and sublime nature of The Lord, as He is The Creator of the seen and the unseen, by Him all things were created that are in Heaven and on earth.

The Epistle came to present an honest picture about our Lord Christ in His Glory and Dignity, for Christ is All in All, and the head of all principality and power (Col. 1: 15-20). He is everything for the believer.

During the days of St. Paul the Apostle, some people believed that Jesus was an abstract person, and that Christ was the Divine Spirit which came upon Him at Baptism and It left Him on the Cross. This means that Christ did not die, but the human Jesus is the one who died. Although they worshipped Christ, they glorified the mediating powers such as the spiritual creatures (1: 16), and worshiped them with Christ.

The Epistle came to affirm the Divinity of The Master, and only in Him there is sufficiency, with no need for other mediators with him.

Some thought that the God of the Old Testament is the Creator of the world and the materials, and Jesus Christ came to free the world from him. Thus, Paul the Apostle revealed that salvation was achieved through Christ, and that it was fulfilled according to the will and love of the Father. He used to always talk about Master Christ and the Father together to destroy any wrong Gnostic inclinations (1: 2, 2: 2).

2. Faith and knowledge:

We have seen that the Gnosticises looked to knowledge (gnosis) as the basics for faith, and that a person through his ability could be saved through his knowledge, which is the fruit of his asceticism and personal struggle. Some Gnosticises considered Christianity as an invitation to ignorance.

In a positive way, Paul the Apostle revealed that knowledge is essential and necessary for our salvation, but it is a gift from the grace of God upon us. The spiritual knowledge which surpasses the human intellect if offered to us by God, He sanctifies and develops it inside us.

Through the work of His Holy Spirit, the Giver of enlightenment, the Apostle frequently repeated the word 'know' or 'knowledge.' He also used to point out to the word 'the secret of God' or 'the secret of Christ' to reveal to us the knowledge hidden even from the heavenlies, which Christ discloses to them and to us.

The Apostle also connects knowledge with 'behaviour in Christ', so that we do not become occupied with theoretical knowledge, but the knowledge of the daily experience through our new practices in Jesus Christ.

3. The Church of social stratification

The Gnosticises believe that the society is divided into two stratifications:

a) The class of the complete: it is not appropriate for those to get married to eat forbidden certain foods, because marriage is defiled and some foods are not pure.

b) The class of the incomplete mediators: they are allowed to get married and to eat whatever they like, because they are weak.

Paul the Apostle removed the stratification difference, talking about Christ and how He reconciles everyone to Himself (1: 20). He frequently repeats 'all' of 'every man' in one verse (1: 28)

4. Doctrine and the behaviour:

This Epistle, in a wonderful way, discloses to us the greatness of the personality of Christ, yet only those who live in Jesus Christ comprehend that greatness, so they collect the riches of His grace and find in Him the true fullness, for it is a doctrinal, practical Epistle.

Christ in our lives

In the Epistle to the Romans, we comprehend that Christ is our righteousness.

In First Corinthians Christ is our richness.

Second Corinthians Christ is our rest.

Galatians Christ is our Redeemer.

Ephesians Christ is our life (we are His Body).

Philippians Christ is our happiness.

In First and Second Thessalonians Christ is coming for our glory.

First Timothy and Titus Christ is our Teacher.

Second Timothy Christ is an Example for us.

Philemon Christ is an Example for us as a Master.

Hebrews Christ is our Atoning Intercessor.

As for the Colossians, Christ is Everything for us, "and you are complete in Him" (Col. 2: 10), we find everything in Him and we are not in need of anything:

• For He is The Light Who saves us from the authority of darkness (1: 12, 13), so that we ourselves become a light to the world.

• He is The Saviour Who saves us from the authority of Satan and every temptation, "in whom we have redemption through His blood, the forgiveness of sins (1: 14).

• He conveys us into His kingdom, i.e., the kingdom of the Son of His love (1: 13). For through Baptism in His Name, we enjoy the sonship of the Father and we are considered the beloved children of the Father.

• As for His Divinity, He is the image of the invisible God (1: 15) in Whom our nature is renewed, so that we become according to His image "and have put on the new man who is renewed in knowledge according to the image of Him who created him" (3: 10). In the first Adam we lost the image of God, and in the Second Adam we regained the image.

• He is the Creator; in Him He had created everything (1: 16). He carried us inside Himself as His Body, He guided us in His light to enjoy His Resurrected life, "who is the beginning, the firstborn from the dead, that in all things He may have the pre-eminence" (1: 18), "For you died, and your life is hidden with Christ in God" (3: 3).

• "And He is the Head of the body, that in all things He may have the pre-eminence. {1: 18}, so that He might be an example for us in everything.

• Through His act of Redemption, He revealed to us the secret of the utmost Divine Love, so we enjoyed hope in the glory, "which is Christ in you, the hope of glory" (1: 27), "When Christ who is our life appears, then you also will appear with Him in glory" (3: 4).

If Gnostic had offended the person of our Lord Christ and made Him as one of the aeons, Paul the Apostle is inviting us to enjoy community with Him in order to experience His sufferings, " now rejoice in my sufferings for you, and fill up in my flesh what is lacking in the afflictions of Christ, for the sake of His body" (1: 24), and His death, "for you died" (3: 3) and His burial, "buried with Him in Baptism" (2: 12), and consequently share in His glory, "then you also will appear with Him in glory" (3: 4). And so, our Master Christ didn't leave us in lack of anything!!

If Gnostic was calling them to mere mental knowledge as the way of salvation, having Christ is the true way, "in whom are hidden all the treasures of wisdom and knowledge." (2: 3).

The Church in Christ

a) The Church is united with Christ because He is its Head (1: 18), through His Incarnation He is not a stranger to it neither it is a stranger to Him, but it is His Body. The origins of this thought came from the words of our Lord Jesus Himself, (Mark 14: 58, John 2: 19, 22). It affixes and unites us with the Lord Christ, as He is the Head of man (1 Cor. 11: 3). Our relationship with Him is that of a spiritual marriage, "For the husband is head of the wife, as also Christ is head of the church; and He is the Saviour of the body." (Eph. 5: 23).

b) Amidst its pains, the Church finds its rest in Christ, as it considers the afflictions filling up what is lacking in the afflictions of Christ, it vouches for the Cross and experiences the sweetness of the community with its Crucified Christ (1: 24).

c) The Master Christ had opened the way for the Church, as He granted it to walk through it (2: 6). Its relationship with Him is a continuous one, which is always working towards fulfilling the deed of its Heavenly Groom. It is rooted and built in Him (2: 7), practicing everything in His Name, especially thanksgiving to God (3: 17, 2: 7).

d) The Church enjoys the fullness in Christ (2: 10). It will not accept anything except to be in His image, and as such, is fulfilled.

e) The Church dies with him (2: 20), is buried with Him (2: 12), is resurrected with Him (3: 1), disappears with Him (3: 3), and appears with Him in glory (3: 4).

f) It took the renewal through the Baptism, and its renewal keeps continuing through the repentance until it completely carries His image (3: 10)

g) It feels rich as the lives of kings, attaining to all riches of the full assurance of understanding, to the knowledge of the mystery of God (2: 2-3, 4: 16)

h) Its Constitution is believing in Christ, the practical love for the brethren, and the hope laid up in Heaven (1: 4-5). This is the key of the Book "Faith, hope and love." This three-sided grace is always connected in the New Testament with the experience of the Christian life. This Constitution is presented in that Book in different ways. The Book came like other Epistles of our teacher Paul the Apostle, declaring the invitation of the Bible, i.e. faith in Christ, in order to love Him in His brethren, and to be present with Him in His Heaven.

i) This Epistle reveals the spirit of the Church and its rejoicing atmosphere. Although the Epistle aims at being cautious of the false teachers, and those of vain philosophies and arrogance, it very clearly announces how the Church should be, having Christ, Its Head Who grants it every richness and fullness, experiencing the authority over Satan and all its powers, as there is no room for darkness inside it anymore. It experiences the joyful Kingdom of God, leading in the kingly way to become an icon of its Creator. That is how the Apostle is offering his experience of the Church, as a rejoicing victorious and glorious life, even amidst sufferings.

j) A rejoicing and victorious life does not push towards idleness and neglect, but towards the serious behaviour in Christ (1: 6), seeking what's in Heaven (3: 12), especially love which is the bond of perfection. In seriousness, the door of the heart will be opened so that the peace of God may rule inside it, practicing the life of perpetual community (3: 15). Our exultant church life pushes us to vigils, together with thanksgiving and preaching the mystery of Christ {4: 2-3}, guiding us in family relationships {3: 18-21}, leading us in our relationships with others {3: 21-25}. It is a life practised at Church, house, work and street, because it is an inner life, its roots are in our depths. It directs our feelings, emotions, powers, talents, words and behaviour. It interferes in every attitude, hidden or unhidden, in other words, our Christianity is to hide in Christ, so we see him in each one, He Himself guides us, and so we enjoy Him.

k) This Epistle reveals that Christianity is a practical invitation to enjoy freedom, as Christ had liberated us from Satan and its darkness, and granted us the sonship of the Father to enjoy His Kingdom, and offered us Himself; The Wisdom. During that freedom, we refuse every invitation to the restrictions of the literal killing and misunderstanding of asceticism, so we serve our Christ as children in glory. This freedom in Christ pushes us towards specific commitments, so this Epistle presents what we should avoid, what we need to struggle in, and how to live thankfully.

The Parts of the Epistle

As the Epistle presents to us the person of Christ, whenever we look, we see Him and we are rooted in Him (1: 2). He is The Everlasting Who carries us to His eternity, granting us the perpetual growth to push us towards Him (2: 7). He is The Life, The Giver of everything (3), He is the Leader of our behaviour.

1- Christ is the Depth

2- Christ is the Height

3- Christ is inside us

4- Christ is the leader of our behaviour

Dimensions of the new life in Christ			
(1)	**(2)**	**(3)**	**(4)**
Christ is the Depth 1: 23	**Christ is the Height**	**Christ is the Glory of the inner life**	**Christ is the Leader of the outer life**
- As a Creator, First born and Head, taking us to the depths to lift us up to the reconciliation with the Father (1: 14-20)	- Above every human philosophy (2: 8)	- Our life is hidden in Him (3: 3)	- He is the Constitution of the family (3: 18-25)
- Through Him we gain the everlasting mystery (1: 2)	- Above the circumcision of the body (2: 11)	- Eternal glory (4: 3)	- He is the Constitution of the group (4: 1)
- Through Him He presents us perfect in wisdom (1: 28)	- Above all the powers of darkness (2: 15)	- It carries His characteristics, especially:	- Our commitment to present Him to the world (4: 5)
	- Above the literal Law (2: 16)	- The love	
	- Above the corners of the world (the dominating spirits) (2: 20)	- The wisdom	
		- Thanksgiving	

Introduction to
THE FIRST EPISTLE TO THE THESSALONIANS

INTRODUCTION AND HISTORY

History of Thessalonica

Thessalonica was the capital of one of the colonies of Macedonia in Greece. Its former name was "Therma," meaning "hot springs." Cassander the First, the son of Antipater, rebuilt it in the year 315 B.C., and made it the centre for his throne. He named the city after his wife, Thessalonica, the sister of Alexander the Great and daughter of Philip II of Macedonia.

In the Roman Empire, it was the capital of the new state, and its population was approximately 200,000. Thessalonica was of great significance due to its geographical location on the Greek route, which is a military road connecting Rome with the East.

The city was a large harbor, equipped as a naval base for the Roman ships with five or six rulers of the city governing it (Acts 17:6). Being a great commercial centre, it attracted many rich Romans and some of the Jewish merchants (Acts 17:4) who held their council there. It was known for its corruption and wickedness, which compelled St. Paul to talk about the life of purity (1 Thess. 4:1-8).

AUDIENCE OF THE EPISTLE

Time and Place of Writing

The epistle to the Thessalonians was likely written towards the end of 52 A.D., or the beginning of 53 A.D., which would have been after a very short period of his ministry in Thessalonica while being in Corinth.

PURPOSE OF THE FIRST EPISTLE TO THE THESSALONIANS

Aim of the Epistle

St. Paul and Silas succeeded in their ministry in Thessalonica, despite only staying for a very short time, "But the Jews who were not persuaded, becoming envious, took some of the evil men from the marketplace, and gathering a mob, set all the city in an uproar and attacked the house of Jason, and sought to bring them out to the people. But when they did not find them, they dragged Jason and some brethren to the rulers of the city, crying out, 'Those who have turned the world upside down have come here too. Jason has harboured them, and these are all acting contrary to the decrees of Caesar, saying there is another king, Jesus" (Acts 17:5-7).

The accusation against Paul and Silas was that they caused an uproar and are against the decrees of Caesar (Acts 17:7). This worried the multitudes and rulers of the city, so they left Thessalonica and went to Berea, but they were attacked also in Berea, so they went to Athens (Acts 17:15), and then to Corinth (Acts 18:1).

The ministry succeeded in Thessalonica between the Jews and the Gentiles. As the Jews stirred their brothers who believed, so the Gentiles stirred their brothers who believed. The church suffered a lot from the Jews and from the Gentiles, and the believers expected St. Paul to go back and help them. But he sent Timothy to strengthen their faith, which made some doubt his fatherhood.

As such, he had to write telling them his desire to see them, declaring his true fatherhood. Moreover, he wanted to draw their attention away from grief and worrying events, and instead towards inner spiritual joy. He talked to them about the resurrection and the advent of the Lord Jesus, to support them amidst their bitter afflictions. He encouraged them in their spiritual strife and for a holy life filled with love, hoping for the eternal crown and the heavenly wedding, so that they may enjoy the Fatherly bosom.

MAIN THEMES AND STRUCTURE OF THE FIRST EPISTLE TO THE THESSALONIANS

Accepting the Faith

St. Paul visited Thessalonica for the first time during his second missionary journey around the year 52 A.D., while Silvanus and Timothy accompanied him (Acts 17:1-10). After being expelled from Philippi, St. Paul directed his attention to the Jews and spoke with them over three Sabbaths in their synagogue. He attracted some of the Jews to the faith, along with many of the proselytes and some of the prominent women. This became the foundation of the first church in Thessalonica.

St. Paul wrote to the Philippians saying, "For even in Thessalonica you sent aid once and again for my necessities" (Phil.4: 16). This reveals he was not relying on the people of Thessalonica financially, and that he stayed there for more than three weeks (1Thess. 2:7-11). He exerted much effort in his ministry, caring for them night and day. Some say that he stayed there more than six months, while others think that he did not stay for more than a month.

Introduction to
THE SECOND EPISTLE TO THE THESSALONIANS

INTRODUCTION AND HISTORY

This epistle, despite its small size, drew the attention and interest of many of the fathers of the early church, such as St. Justin the martyr, St. Erinaos, St. Clement of Alexandria and the scholar Tertullian. What was so interesting about this epistle, was the obvious prophecy by St. Paul the apostle about the great apostasy or (falling away) through the appearance of the "man of sin" or the "son of perdition." This represents an embodiment of Satan, opposing the spiritual kingdom of the Lord Christ at the end of ages. This epistle preoccupied many of the scholars and critics of the Holy Book; some of them dismissed its authenticity, others its reference to the apostle Paul, and still others, although accepting its authenticity and its reference to the apostle Paul, believe that it actually precedes the other one, meaning it is his first and not his second epistle to the Thessalonians. Many scholars came forward to rebut those critics, confirming the soundness of the traditional thought of the church with regards to its authenticity, its reference to the apostle Paul, and that it is his second, not the first, epistle to the Thessalonians.

Authenticity of the Epistle

The early church has for a long time been consistent with looking at this epistle as an integral part of the word of God inspired by the Holy Spirit, and that its holiness is indisputable. Many of the fathers of the church in the second century A.D. quoted it in their works, including St. Augustine, St. Barnabas, St. Justin the martyr, and St. Polycarpos the 'Dedakia.' There are even some texts which go back to the first century A.D., with many significant people quoting from it, such as in the writings of St. Erinaos, St. Clement of Alexandria, and the scholar Tertullian, of the second century A.D. It was mentioned in the law of Mercion, was referred to among the epistles of the apostle Paul in the 'Mortarian List' and was included in the old Latin and Syrian versions.

AUDIENCE AND AUTHOR OF THE EPISTLE

Time and Place of Writing

It seems that it was written and sent from Corinth a few months after the first one, in about the year 72 A.D., when St. Timothy and St. Silas was still with St. Paul (1:1).

The Author of the Epistle

There were no doubts raised during the early centuries concerning the authorship of this epistle. It carried in itself strong evidence that the apostle Paul is its author. For example, it referred to the author on more than one occasion (1: 1; 3: 17). It also bore St. Paul's signature writing style, as far as its overall form is concerned. The apostle Paul used to begin most of his epistles by mentioning his name, those to whom it is addressed, the apostolic blessing, thanksgiving to God for every success or growth he sees in them, and a mention of support to encourage them. He then enters into the main topic, which deals with faith, doctrine, and behaviour aspects, finally ending it with practical commandments and a conclusive word.

Besides the fact that this overall form overtly present within this epistle, it also demonstrates the features of the personality of this great apostle: his delicacy, his flaming zeal toward the salvation of mankind, his care to pray for the sake of others, and to seek their prayers for his own sake. All of these things combined proclaim that this epistle is the product of the unique and flaming mind of the apostle Paul.

Other than these forms of evidence, there are also external testimonies mentioned by the fathers of the early church, who, from the beginning, quoted it as an authentic book and considered it as the living word of God. The scholars Origen and Josabius testified that it has been widely known all over the world during their days

Objections to its Authenticity

The scholars, defending the authenticity of this epistle, and its reference to the apostle Paul, noticed that the objections of its critics are so weak and not strong enough to stand before the traditional thought of the church. We can summarise the main objections in the following points:

a) The main objection is the eschatological differences between the two epistles. In the first epistle to the Thessalonians (4:12; 5:11), in an attempt to prepare the minds of believers to the spiritual watching and strife in anticipation for when we, who are alive, will be caught up together with those who are asleep to encounter the Lord coming on the clouds, to be forever with them. The apostle hints that the day of the Lord is at hand, that it will come unexpectedly as a thief in the night, and as labour pains upon a pregnant woman. By contrast, in the second epistle to the same congregation, he confirms that day will not come unless preceded by an obvious sign, when the apostasy (the rebellion) occurs, and 'the man of sin, the son of perdition" is revealed, who opposes and exalts himself above God in His Church and show himself that he is God (2 Thessalonians 2:1-4).

Looking deeply into these two epistles, we shall find no difference in thought, but only difference in the circumstance that prevailed around each of them, that led the apostle to include a certain aspect of the eschatological thought and not the other. What came in the two epistles are actually not two opposing thoughts, but rather two integral aspects of the same faith thought.

To explain this, we may say that in his first epistle to the Thessalonians, intending to encourage them to lead a life of watching and strife without murmur but with a perpetual thanksgiving amid the tribulation, the apostle concentrated on the element of suddenness of the coming of the ultimate day of the Lord. He did this in order to inflame the longing of those who spiritually strive, to work with joy and sure hope and at the same time, to warn those slothful and confused, lest they might fall and be deprived of the blessing and joy of the everlasting encounter with the Groom of their souls, coming to them.

In the second epistle, addressed to the same congregation, the apostle writes with a new and an additional goal; namely, the necessity of walking with wisdom and prudence in this world. This was done so either out of misunderstanding of the first epistle, or because they probably received another epistle wrongly referred to the apostle. Some of those believers, assuming that the ultimate coming of the Lord is at hand, sold their possessions and others stopped their daily activities in anticipation of the day of the Lord, that will come any day. This was something that caused a great state of confusion and chaos in the whole Church. That is why the apostle hastened to write to them this second epistle, to warn them against those actions against faith and to confirm that the day of the Lord will not come before certain obvious public signs precede them--specifically the appearance of "the man of sin, the son of perdition."

Therefore, the elements in both epistles are not two contradictory thoughts, but represent one integral thought which appears very obviously in a long talk by the Lord Christ Himself about the signs that will precede His ultimate coming, including the appearance of the antichrist; referring at the same time to the element of suddenness, and to our anticipation of the times and seasons (Mark 13; Matthew 24; Luke 7; Acts 1).

b) Some scholars attempted to attribute what was in the second epistle about the ultimate coming of the Lord and the appearance of the man of sin, to a later era than that of the apostle Paul. They claim that the second epistle to the Thessalonians is not written by him, but that its real author has quoted thought from the book of revelations written by St. John the evangelist. The man of sin, according to some of them, refers to the reappearance of the tyrant emperor Nero, about whom it was claimed that he did not die but hid somewhere in the East, where he prepares himself to appear anew to resume his opposition against the Church and her faith in the Lord Christ. Others claimed that the man of sin was Vespasian, and still others claimed that he represents the era of Trajan.

Such objection could not be well received, as what is similar to this thought of the man of sin goes even as far back as the prophet Daniel (Daniel 11), which was obviously known in the Jewish documents preceding Christianity. It was also clearly proclaimed by the Lord Christ Himself, in the gospel according to St. Mark (Chapter 13).

In another way, the apostle Paul in his preaching the gospel, faced continuous opposition, and even in his days many apostates from faith appeared, that by his fiery heart and his spiritual insight which was inspired by the Holy Spirit. A movement of apostasy, much more violent and bitter than that through which the Church was passing in his days, will directly precede the ultimate coming of the Lord Christ, in which Satan will be embodied in the person of the son of perdition, opposing the person of Christ, until the measure of evil is consummated.

c) Besides these two objections, some critics claim that while the first epistle is characterised by abundant and warm feelings of the apostle toward the Thessalonians, the second epistle, on the other hand, is almost formal and firm. In the first epistle he says, "We give thanks to God always for you all" (1 Thessalonians 1:2); while in the second one he says, "We are bound to give thanks to God always for you" (2 Thessalonians 1:3; 2:13); ... "We command you" ... and "Those who are such, we command and exhort through our Lord Jesus Christ ..." (2 Thessalonians 3:6, 13). But we can attribute this change in the way of speech to a change in its goal. The apostle wrote this first epistle like a father writing to encourage his children in a time of tribulation, demonstrating his compassionate fatherhood and revealing his partaking of their sufferings. Whereas in the second one, although he is writing to the same congregation, he commands and exhorts them because of their erroneous behaviour and their slothful abstaining from their daily work. We actually cannot ask the apostle to write all of his epistles with the same tone, as he must change it according to the difference in issues and the circumstances prevailing at the time.

The second difference with which critics concentrated on, was according to a suggestion by A Hamack. They stated that the first epistle was addressed more to the believers of the Gentile origin, whereas the second one was addressed more to those who have great knowledge of the Old Testament. Such a theory of a divided Church in the same province, into a church of the Gentiles and one of the converted Jews, is totally unacceptable. This is especially true seeing that the apostle Paul who is a great believer in the unity of the Church, demands in his first epistle, "I charge you by the Lord that this epistle be read to all the holy brethren" (1 Thessalonians 5:27), with no discernment between those of Jewish origin and those of Gentile origin. Quoting the Old

Testament does not imply that it is addressed to those of Jewish origin, as the gospels which were written to those of Gentile origin, like that according to St. Mark, include several quotations from the Old Testament.

D) Some critics in their allegations note that the differences between the two epistles work as evidence for their objections to the second epistle. Moreover, some were of the opinion that the great similarity, particularly in the opening preface, which is almost the same in both of them, is rather an evidence that raises doubt in the authenticity of the second epistle, saying that there is no need for the apostle to write another epistle to the same congregation within such a short interval of time and with such similar issues.

This objection is very weak, however, as the two epistles carry both significant similarities and differences. What is similar between them is the apostle's confirmation of certain issues that need to be addressed, whereas the difference between them is when he writes about something new that happened after writing the first epistle.

Going through those objections, we are more convinced of the authenticity of this epistle, of its true reference to the apostle Paul. There is no significant point in the attempts made by certain scholars to suggest its reference to an unknown author, or to that it is written by St. Timothy and St. Silas and only signed by the apostle Paul (2 Thessalonians 3:17),or that it is an epistle especially addressed to the Church of the Jewish origin. As these solutions stir up many problems, the majority of scholars were committed to the true thought of the Church.

PURPOSE OF THE SECOND
EPISTLE TO THE THESSALONIANS

The Aim of the Epistle

As we already said, the main goal of sending this epistle was to correct the wrong concepts into which some believers have fallen, concerning the ultimate coming of the Lord. Assuming that His coming is at hand, they hastened to be slothful in their daily life and to walk without order. That is why he wrote to confirm to them that the coming of the Lord has to be preceded by the appearance of the son of perdition, which will cause a great apostasy (2 Thessalonians 2:3).

It appears that because a certain message was wrongly referred to him, it provided to them some wrong concepts concerning the ultimate coming of the Lord. As such, St. Paul hastened to send them this epistle, signed by him (3:17), to correct the misunderstanding.

As the Church was still under tribulation, he wrote to them in a fatherly way, to encourage them to endure the sufferings, and to demonstrate to them how to walk as is befitting the children of God.

MAIN THEMES AND STRUCTURE
OF THE SECOND EPISTLE TO THE THESSALONIANS

The Order of Writing of the Two Epistles

Some scholars, contrary to the true Church tradition, claim that the second epistle preceded the other one. They claim this using a few different types of evidence, which were all rejected by the majority of scholars on account of their weaknesses and lack of conviction.

Some claim that the order in which these two epistles came in the book was not according to their fate of sending, but according to their respective size. This view, however, is unacceptable, especially seeing that they came in this same order in the law of Mercion, which does not care for the size of the holy books.

Some believe that the first epistle contains nothing that is too difficult to understand that would warrant sending another epistle to interpret. Yet, this view is also unacceptable on account of the fact that the talk of the apostle in the first epistle (1 Thessalonians 4:13; 5:11) concerning the ultimate coming of the Lord Christ, has been misunderstood. He hastened to write to them about the signs that precede His coming (2 Thessalonians 2:1-11), to consummate what came in the first epistle, and to correct the misunderstanding thereof.

Some scholars believe that the first epistle talked about the conquest of the Thessalonians (1 Thessalonians 1:6-8) as though the crisis has already come to an end, while the second one talks about the anguish, which still prevails and even expected in the future. This evidence is unacceptable as well, as the talk of the apostle about a conquest and victory does not imply the end of anguish but is rather to encourage and support them to consummate their strife and to exhort them to receive the suffering with more thanksgiving. Gaining conquest does not mean the end of the spiritual war, nor imply the cessation of anguish, as another will always follow the conquest, all the time.

Some scholars believe that the apostle in the first epistle seems to be quite aware of the inner circumstances of the Church of Thessalonians, saying, "concerning brotherly love, you have no need that I should write to you, for you yourselves are taught by God to love one another... and indeed you do so" (1 Thessalonians 4:9-10). While, in the second epistle he writes as though he needs to know how they are doing, saying, "we have confidence in the Lord concerning you, both that you do and will do the things we command you" (2 Thessalonians 3:4-5).

In response to this objection, we say that because the apostle wrote his first epistle to encourage and support them amid their anguish, he demonstrated their good side, confirming that their spiritual tendency, which he knows for sure, would make them grow more and more. However, in the second one, he wrote to enquire and make sure that they are walking along the sound path, after such misunderstanding of the issue of the ultimate coming of the Lord.

Some object that in the first epistle he wrote to them saying, "Concerning the times and the seasons, brethren, you have no need that I should write to you" (1 Thessalonians 5:1); then, in the second one, he revealed the appearance of the man of sin (2 Thessalonians 2:3). According to them, it would be more logical to write in the first one about the man of sin and when they come to ask about the time and season of his appearance, in order to fix the time of the ultimate coming of the Lord, he would then tell them that they have no need to know the times and season.

In response to this objection, we say that the apostle Paul while preaching to them, spoke about the anticipated coming of the Lord. Then after leaving them, a serious debate stirred up about the time of the Lord's coming and the appearance of his everlasting kingdom – a natural debate that has even come in the minds of the disciples of the Lord (Matthew 24:3), and still comes in the minds of Christians, east and west, up to this very day; caused by man's anticipation of the future events, and his inner longing for knowledge. As the Lord Christ did with His disciples, the apostle Paul also did with the Thessalonians; He first exhorted them that instead of being preoccupied by the need to know the times and seasons, they should watch and be prepared for the coming of the Lord. Then, having misunderstood his talk, he wrote to them about the appearance of the man of sin, not in an attempt to fix the time and season, but rather to correct their misunderstanding.

Some scholars noticed that the apostle Paul in his first epistle to the Thessalonians, started some topics with the word "But" (4:9; 5:1); which implies that he is continuing on something that he wrote before, saying therefore, that this is not the first epistle but must be preceded by another one. Other scholars say that this does not mean a commitment by the apostle to send an epistle preceding that one, but instead refers to the fact that he might have already dealt with these topics before, even orally, while preaching to them, or that he is presenting his own view in the Lord after some other minister might have already done.

His conclusive remark, "I, Paul, write this greeting with my own hand. This is the mark in every letter of mine; it is the way I write" (2 Thessalonians 3:17), should be written in his first epistle. Therefore, this epistle is not the second one, but the first. Saying that the apostle following the confusion between the authentic could rebut that and the false epistle wrongly referred to him wrote this remark.

As it was written in the first epistle that he sent Timothy to them (1 Thessalonians 3:2), some believe that this refers to this epistle being written after sending Timothy, who carried the second epistle with him, therefore proving that this second epistle is in fact the first one.

This can be rebutted by saying that the apostle did not send Timothy as a courier of messages, but as a "fellow labourer in the gospel of Christ, to establish (you) and encourage (you) concerning (your) faith." Moreover, if it was Timothy who carried the epistle in our hands, he would have been referred to as such in the epistle.

The scholars did not stop at responding to the objection of those claiming that it is the first and not the second epistle of the apostle Paul to the Thessalonians. They also referred to the following positive aspects to confirm the authentic thought of the Church concerning the order of the two epistles:

1. That the problems came in the first epistle came in the second one, deeper, or as a consummation to them.

2. That in the second epistle, the apostle obviously refers to the fact that he has sent them a previous one (2:2; 3:17); which we can assume is the first epistle, while in the first epistle, he did not refer to the one before it.

3. If the epistle in our hands is the first one, how would he exhort and warn in it, then send another one carrying personal warm feelings? The usual process of the apostle Paul is to start by giving love and warm emotions, to prepare the listener or reader to accept the exhortation and warning that would follow.

Introduction to
THE FIRST EPISTLE TO TIMOTHY

INTRODUCTION AND HISTORY

Who was Timothy?

Timothy is a Greek name that means "righteous man of God," or "The honour of God." Timothy believed in Christ through St. Paul during his first preaching journey in Lystra of Iconium, in 46 A.D. His father was a Greek whose name is unknown, and who likely died when Timothy was still very young. His mother, Eunice, and his grandmother, Lois, were Jews and they were the ones who brought him up. Both of them taught him the Holy Scripture (2 Timothy 1:5, 3:15) but they did not circumcise him. It was, however, St. Paul who circumcised him, in order to avoid the wrath of the Jews (Acts 16:22). During this second missionary journey, St. Paul found him in good faith and spiritual enthusiasm (1 Timothy 1:18).

Timothy was known to be pious among the believers (Acts 16:2). Therefore, the apostle chose him to accompany him in his journey. He travelled with the apostle to Galatia, Troas, Philippi and Thessalonica. However, Timothy stayed in Berea with Silas when the apostle left it suddenly (Acts 17:14). Later on, he joined St Paul in Macedonia and

Corinth and it seems that he stayed with him during his stay in Corinth. Then, St Paul sent him with Erastus to Macedonia before his third journey (Acts 19:22). Timothy is mentioned in the prologues of Paul's epistles (2 Cor 1:1; Phili 1:1; 1 Cor 1:1; 1 Thess 1:2; 2 Thess 1:1, Phil 1). His name is also mentioned in the final farewell in the epistle to the Romans (16:21).

Timothy was sent to Corinth by St. Paul because of the turbulence that took place before the writing of the first letter (1 Cor 16:10). St Paul also pointed to Timothy's contributions with him in spreading the Gospel in Corinth (2 Cor 1:19). Upon writing the letter to the Philippians, Timothy was sent to Philippi (Phil 2:19). He was also sent to Thessalonica to write a report before the writing of the first letter to its believers (1 Thess 3:2, 6). In the letter to the Hebrews (Heb 13:23), the apostle Paul points to Timothy's imprisonment and release.

It seems that after Paul's first release from his first imprisonment in 63 A.D., he left St. Timothy to care for affairs in Ephesus. From all this, we can see the close relationship that existed between St. Paul and his disciple, and the full confidence he had in him. Many times, St. Paul calls Timothy 'My son,' 'My true son,' 'My dear son' or 'My trusted son' (1 Tim 1:2;18; 1 Cor 4:17; 2 Tim 1:2). By reading the expressions used in the two epistles to Timothy, it seems that he was shy by nature and that he suffered from poor health.

AUTHENTICITY OF THE EPISTLE

External Evidence

During the second century A.D., around the year 170 A.D., the Muratorian Canon, which is considered the oldest formal list of the New Testament, mentions the 13 epistles of St. Paul and so omits the Epistle to the Hebrews. In that same period, the Paschito Canon mentions St. Paul's 14 epistles, including the Pastoral epistles as legally acknowledged books. Eusebius also mentions such epistles with St. Paul's other writings as acknowledged and confirmed legal books.

None of the eastern or western Church fathers doubted the authenticity of these epistles, or that their author was any other than St. Paul the Apostle. Indeed, many of the church fathers have used many quotations from these epistles in their writings. Examples can be seen in the writings of St. Clement the Roman, St. Theophilus of Antioch, St. Irenaeus, Tertullian and St. Clement of Alexandria. The latter borrowed from the first and second epistles to Timothy when he wrote about the heretics who had refuted tem since they revealed their misunderstanding and ignorance of S.t Paul's teachings. He also borrowed from St. Paul's epistle to Titus.

Internal evidence

This is not less powerful than the external one. Starting from the 19th century, some critics began attacking these epistles. They refused the fact that St. Paul is their author and consequently refused their legality. They based their opposition on historical, ecclesiastic, traditional and linguistic reasons. It is possible to present a summary of the most important points in their criticism as follows:

Firstly, from a historic viewpoint, their protests alleged that such epistles could not be identified with any part of St. Paul's life as it is related in the book of Acts. We can answer such objections by saying that the Apostle's life and work cannot be limited to what is mentioned in the Book of Acts. Concerning what is written at the end of that Book about the Apostle's imprisonment, we know that this was not the last chapter in his life. We also know that he was released to preach until he was imprisoned again in Rome, and that he was martyred during the reign of Nero.

The Acts of the Apostles mentions that the governor Felix, Festus and Agrippa did not find anything that would enable them to condemn the apostle Paul and imprison or kill him. He could have been released if he had not appealed to Caesar (Acts 26:31-32). Therefore, when he was sent to Rome, he was released. This is what we find in the apostle's writings since he expected himself to be released (Phil 1:25-2:24, Phil

22). This appears also in the church tradition embodied in the writings of the historian Eusebius.

On the other hand, many of the dangers that the apostle was exposed to and which he mentions in the second letter to the Corinthians (2:24-27), are not mentioned in Acts. Moreover, in the second century, the Muratorian Document speaks about St. Paul's journey to Spain, which is an event that did not take place before the apostle's first imprisonment in Rome. Therefore, we cannot limit the life and work of St Paul to what is mentioned in the Acts, whether they are events that have taken place preceding his imprisonment at the end of the book or after. The apostle undertook his missionary work, preached and wrote his pastoral epistles during the last period of his life.

Secondly, from a doctrinal viewpoint, some critics see differences between the thought expressed by the apostle in his epistles and those in his other writings. They see that even if the pastoral epistles have some paulistic thoughts, such thoughts are exceptions. Instead of a belief in the Trinity: faith in the Father who opens his fatherly bosom, in the Son through whom we become rich, holy and righteous and in the Holy Spirit that takes us to participate in the glories and the blessing of free grace, St. Paul talks about the life of piety and good acts. Mcgiffent talks about these epistles as not having any trace of the main great truth found in the other writings of St. Paul, specifically the death of the physical body and life in the spirit.

We can respond to these critics by saying that these epistles were written by St. Paul in his old age. He was satisfied with his earlier teachings concerning edification and tradition, and he knew that they had become widely spread in all churches. Therefore, there was no need for repetition since the Christian belief was clear. On the other hand, the Epistles were not intended for the people of a church, but they were directed to pastors. They clearly convey a pastoral aim and underline ecclesiastical orders and Christian behaviour. We can call them farewell epistles to Church servants, to whom the apostle delivers pastoral responsibility and ministry.

Thirdly, some protestors claim that the apostle focuses in these epistles upon the ecclesiastical orders, the ordination bishops and deacons, and the designation of the role of widows etc. which, in their view, did not occupy the mind and heart of the apostles that yearns for the second advent of Jesus Christ. They stated that in his previous epistles, the apostle did not speak about organisational details. He was interested in inflaming the spiritual capabilities of each individual. Such critics find that the orders were instituted much later on and after the era of St. Paul. These allegations can be answered as follows:

1. It is true that the writings of St Paul in particular and those of the Early Church in general, tended to deal with eschatological issues. All were looking forward eagerly and anxiously to the second and last advent of Christ. However, this attitude did not mean that the Church ignored the importance of ecclesiastical orders. On the contrary, when St. Paul wrote his first letter to the Thessalonians, he talked about the coming of Christ. However, when he found out that they had misunderstood it and thought that His Advent had come, leaving their daily works because of it, St. Paul hurried to correct their misunderstanding. He stressed the necessity of adhering to order and organisation as well as to daily work (2 Thess 2:6-15). Moreover, he asked them to avoid mingling with those who live without order. If this applies to individuals, how much more would this be required of the Church? It becomes clearly essential for her to live in order and organisation in all aspects of her pastoral life and worship as she awaits the advent of her bridegroom.

2. St Paul believed in the principle of "unity of life", and so he did not accept duality. The Christian lives as a heavenly and earthly citizen simultaneously, without any conflict or contradiction between his heavenly spiritual life and his daily practical one. The believer believes in the unit of life in Christ without confusion between heavenly thoughts and life on earth, or between sanctifying the spirit and the body as well. Similarly, the Church as one sanctified whole knows but one life in Christ. Hence, there is no contradiction between the Church order

and spiritual life. If the apostle is spiritually inflamed and inspired, not occupied to speak in detail about the Church order in his early epistles, this does not indicate that he belittles or ignores such matters, for spirituality does not mean disorder or confusion.

3. Concerning the claim that such church order took place at a much later period, this is not true. Deacons existed directly after the start of the early church on the holy day of the Pentecost (Acts 6). St. Luke, in his accounts in the Acts about the journeys of the apostle Paul and his preaching, tells us that Paul and Barnabas "had appointed elders for them in each Church (Acts 14:23). The apostle Paul also directed one of his epistles from captivity to the people including bishops and deacons (Phil 1:1). In his letter to the Romans, the apostle recommends the deaconess to the church, Phoebe (Romans 16:1).

Fourthly, some of the objections raised as mentioned, are made in the Pastoral epistles of the false teachers. These are the Gnostics who lived during the second century at a period, which comes much later after the apostle. The truth is that the teachers mentioned by Paul are people whose majority called for a return to the literal application of the law, especially to the practice of physical circumcision. On the other hand, if Gnosticism had risen during the second century with its prominent leaders, Gnostic thought preceded Christianity and affected both paganism and Judaism. Indeed, its roots and beginnings appeared during the age of the apostles.

Fifthly, the Pastoral Epistles were not mentioned in Macion's list, published in the second century. This is natural because the list does not represent the ecclesiastical thought of the Orthodox Church. Marcion deleted even the holy gospels such as Matthew, Mark and John. Perhaps he had not received these epistles. This is doubtful, however, as it is likely that Marcion had known them, but not accepted them since they opposed and challenged his Gnostic thought. For example, they spoke about the Law as being good (1 Tim 1:8), whereas Marcion rejected the Old Testament as a whole. Besides, St. Paul's epistles encourage the resistance to false teachings (1 Tim 6:20).

Sixthly, from a linguistic viewpoint, some see that the pastoral epistles have 902 Greek words, 306 of which do not occur in his other epistles. This is natural, since such epistles have a completely different aim from that of the other epistles. In his other epistles, St. Paul wrote to specific churches to deal with theological issues and ecclesiastical disputes. In the Pastoral Epistles, he wrote to pastors about their pastoral work and church orders. Therefore, they had to have their own features and relevant expressions and words. So, we cannot say linguistic differences indicate a different writer. It indicates different issues. Moreover, such epistles include 50 Greek words that are mentioned in St. Paul's other epistles, but which do not appear in any other New Testament book.

Finally, we can say with N.J. White that those epistles possess Paulistic characteristics, for they embody his style, his seriousness, and his spiritual power. They reflect his loving spiritual strength and purity that is coupled with great courage and holiness. Moreover, these epistles are similar to his other epistles in their general framework, in that they have a prologue, apostolic blessing, core of the issue, and epilogue. They also convey his general inclination to resist any return to the literal obedience of the law.

AUDIENCE OF THE EPISTLE

Time and Place of Writing

It was written approximately in the year 64 or 65 A.D., after the release of St. Paul from his first imprisonment in the spring of 63 A.D. He wrote it when he was on his way, passing through Macedonia and after he had visited Ephesus (1 Tim 1:3).

PURPOSE OF THE FIRST EPISTLE TO TIMOTHY

Aim of the Epistle

St. Paul sent the epistle to Timothy to clarify his pastoral commitments in Ephesus. He tells him about certain church orders concerning general procedures of worship and the characteristics of pastors as well as their duties, especially those dealing with the constant struggle against fighting devious heresies. Finally, he focuses on the pastoral relationships that connect the pastor with all the different types of masses.

MAIN THEMES AND STRUCTURE OF THE FIRST EPISTLE TO TIMOTHY

Special Features

These epistles are neither private nor personal ones. They are actually essays that lay down the general basis of evangelical work through which we can sense the characteristics of the early Church. They are characterised with practicality, especially concerning the pastoral aspect during the apostolic age, without dealing with theological and faith problems.

The First Epistle to Timothy closely resembles the Epistle to Titus, as both were directed to two pastors (bishops) dedicated to a new service in Ephesus and Crete. The second epistle to Timothy has a different purpose, which is to support the Church against Emperor Nero's persecution and the imprisonment of St Paul in Rome awaiting his martyrdom.

Different from the other New Testament books, these epistles deal with the Church order during the apostolic age. They are directed to every pastor, as he is considered "a spiritual soldier for Christ." He lawfully struggles to preserve the faith handed down to him by the apostles without deviation--pure from heresies and false teachings. They also draw attention to the necessity or positive work and service and the avoidance of confusion, which results from unfruitful arguments.

Introduction to
THE SECOND EPISTLE
TO TIMOTHY

INTRODUCTION AND HISTORY

This epistle has a very special significance, as our teacher St. Paul, the Apostle to the Gentiles, has written to his most beloved disciple St. Timothy. He was his partner in the pastoral ministry and St. Paul had ordained him Bishop of Ephesus. This epistle is the last one St. Paul had written from his second imprisonment, where he was waiting for the day of his martyrdom. He longed to meet with his disciple in order to deliver him his final advice. As he feared that he would not have time, St. Paul poured his heart as a minister, and recorded his farewell advice to his very special son, St. Timothy.

Background History of the Epistle

From this epistle, it appears that St. Paul wrote it while he was in prison in Rome (1:8,16; 4:6). The year may have been 67 or 68 A.D. approximately, during his second imprisonment and not the first. St. Paul during this time was imprisoned twice: the first time he was held inside the prison, whereas in the second time he was living in an apartment he was renting, but was under "house arrest" and not in an actual prison.

There are a few reasons which indicate that this epistle was written during his second imprisonment. Firstly, he did not expect to be released soon or to leave Rome. This is different from what he says in his epistle to the Philippians (1:24, 2:24), or in his epistle to Philemon (22). On the contrary, here he is expecting martyrdom. He says, "For I am already being poured out as a drink offering, and the time of my departure is at hand." (4:6).

Some explain that the apostle here is referring to his first imprisonment and the trial which ended in his release and return to the ministry, as he says, "At my first defense no one stood with me, but all forsook me. May it not be charged against them. But the Lord stood with me and strengthened me, so that the message might be preached fully through me, and that all the Gentiles might hear. And I was delivered out of the mouth of the lion." (4:16-17). However, most scholars find that the apostle is speaking here about the expected appearance before the Roman emperor, Nero, at a certain time, and that the case had been postponed. He also indicated how the ministry became fervent between the two trials and while he was in prison.

The apostle asks St. Timothy to bring him the robe that he had left in Troas with Carpus (4:13), as well as the books, especially the parchment. This indicated that the apostle was arrested by a Roman order, upon Nero's demand and at an unexpected time. Therefore, he had no chance to gather his belongings.

AUDIENCE OF THE EPISTLE

Who was this Epistle for?

St. Paul wrote this epistle to St. Timothy, who was preaching in Ephesus where he shepherded the congregation. Evidence of this could be noted as follows:

1. He asks him to greet Onesiphorus (2 Tim 4:19), who was in Ephesus (1:18)

2. He charges him to pass by Troas on his way to Rome (4:13). Now this city was situated on the concrete road that stretched from Ephesus to Rome, as we understand from the passage in the Acts of the Apostles (20:5; 2 Cor 2:12)

3. He warns him from Alexander the coppersmith (4:14), who was in Ephesus (Acts 19:33; 1 Tim 1:20)

4. He commands him to "come to him quickly" (4:9) and adds, "And Tychicus I have sent to Ephesus" (4:12). It seems that St. Paul has sent him there to replace St. Timothy during his absence in Rome.

5.The deviations and errors that St. Paul encourages St. Timothy to resist, are the same as the ones he mentions in his first epistle. It is as though St. Timothy will receive this second epistle in the same city of Ephesus where he had received the first epistle.

PURPOSE OF THE SECOND EPISTLE TO TIMOTHY

The Aim of the Epistle

The apostle writes to his disciple to ask him to go to him and bring St Mark too. He wishes to see them whilst in prison and before his martyrdom and fears he will die before their arrival. Consequently, he presents in this epistle a final farewell as well as some fatherly advice. He underlines the necessity of struggling in a spirit of strength, rather than of pessimism. This is important to preserve the upright faith and to oppose the heresies with firmness, coupled with gentleness and love. He also encourages them to teach others who are needed to support the ministry.

The apostle writes while he is expecting to die in Rome. He writes to a church that is suffering under the yoke of the unjust Nero. Therefore, he writes to encourage the Church to bear the pain without complaining or doubting. He repeats the expression "do no be ashamed", since affliction does not confine the word but drives many to work without feeling ashamed of the Cross of our Lord Jesus Christ.

This epistle comes from a victorious servant who bids farewell to a world full of affliction. He announced that he has completed the struggle and has kept the faith entrusted to him until the last breath, and now awaits the eternal crown.

MAIN THEMES AND STRUCTURE OF THE SECOND EPISTLE TO TIMOTHY

Some of the names mentioned in the epistles St. Paul has written while he was in prison for the first time, are names of people who were with him at that time. These do not appear in this second epistle, and this indicates that the epistle has been written while he was in prison for the second time. For example, in his epistle to the Colossians, St. Paul mentions that Timothy, Mark and Demas are with him (Col 1:1; 4:1, 14). By contrast, in the second epistle, he is writing to St. Timothy who is living in Ephesus, and he asks him to bring along St. Mark the apostle (4:11). He also says that Demas has abandoned him (4:10)

Introduction to
THE EPISTLE
TO TITUS

INTRODUCTION AND HISTORY

How the Gospel Entered into the Island of Crete

In the book of Acts, we read that some Cretans were present in Jerusalem on the day of Pentecost (2:11), and those among them who believed returned home to preach the word. However, no fruition of that preaching was recorded in the Holy Book, nor in history. On his way to Rome, the prisoner St. Paul (Acts 27: 7,8) was not met by any Cretan Christians, which led some to confirm that until his first imprisonment, ministry in this island was of no significant weight.

Some believe that after his first imprisonment in Rome, the apostle Paul returned to Asia Minor and Macedonia, maybe even crossing over into Crete, where he stayed long enough for his preaching to reach many towns, to warrant the ordination of many bishops, and for Titus to stay there as the head bishop.

In that same trip, the apostle left his disciple, Timothy, in Ephesus, and went to Macedonia where from there (or maybe from a neighbouring town close to Nicopolis), he wrote to his two disciples, Timothy and Titus.

AUDIENCE OF THE EPISTLE

Who is Titus?

It is claimed that he was from Antioch in Syria; a nephew of the ruler of the island of Crete and was a gentile (Galatians 2:3), born to Gentile parents. He was converted to Christianity at the hand of the apostle Paul, who called him "his true son" (1:4) and who was someone in his close circle who preached under his supervision. According to St John Chrysostom: having been one of the apostle's favourites, he entrusted him with the burden of the entire island; to set in order the things that were lacking it (1:5); and to make him overseer over many bishops.

We do not know when, where, or how he believed; all we know is that he believed through the hands of the apostle Paul fourteen years after his transformation, and then moved around together with him. Titus accompanied him to Jerusalem (Galatians 2:1) and attended the first council of the apostles in Jerusalem (Acts 15), where his presence had a special significance being a living testament of the work of God among the Gentiles.

After the council, he probably returned to Antioch with the two apostles, Paul and Barnabas, together with Silas and Judas (Acts 15:23). It was obvious that because the apostle Paul felt comfortable with his company, he took him wherever he went. Titus was with him in Crete, where he was left to set in order the things that were lacking, and to ordain bishops and priests. This likely occurred after the apostle's first imprisonment.

Titus was also with him during his second imprisonment, although he did not stay till the tribunal, but left for Dalmatia (2 Corinthians 4:10). According to tradition, he returned to Crete, where he preached in it and in the neighbouring islands.

St. Eronimus claims that he departed at 94 years of age; and stayed a virgin his whole life, and that the people of Venice, having preached among them, revere him greatly.

Time and Place of Writing

Some believe that the apostle Paul wrote from Ephesus, whereas others believe that it was written from Nicopolis, after his imprisonment in the year 63 or 64 A.D.

PURPOSE OF THE EPISTLE TO TITUS

The Aim of the Epistle

The island of Crete, a Mediterranean island halfway between Egypt and Italy, about 140 miles long and 35 miles wide; having been known since the old times for corruption and for the appearance of false teachers who proclaimed Jewish fables; the apostle Paul wrote this epistle to encourage his disciple bishop Titus to war against every false teaching; and to "preach, exhort, and rebuke with authority; and to let no one despise him" (2:15).

MAIN THEMES AND STRUCURE OF THR EPISTLE TO TITUS

Significance of the Epistle

The apostle Paul wrote this epistle to his disciple 'Titus', the bishop responsible for the entire island of Crete. Having been known for his upright faith and blameless behaviour according to the spirit of the church, this epistle did not come to establish a faith doctrine, nor to correct certain theological thoughts, but to demonstrate the upright faith in the life of that particular bishop.

This epistle revealed to us an important aspect and a deep contemplation of the Christian life, in that it is not mere mental doctrines, nor controversial philosophies, but is rather a life and a spirit by which the bishop lives, as well as the layman--each within his own responsibility and work. We can say that this epistle represents for us the apostolic thought concerning the shepherding work, which concentrates in the following tasks:

Ordainment of bishops, priests, deacons

The head bishop should not bow his back to bear the yoke of Christ all by himself, but in love, should seek other shepherds and ministers to partake of his love for Christ in his shepherding and preaching mission. It has been the spirit of the early church, to instigate all energies to work: those with a leadership talent, virgins, widows, elders and even children; all should practice the spirit of ministering in some way or another. Yet neither the volume of work, nor the multitude of ministers is important, but great caution and elaboration should be followed, particularly in electing the priest. This should be considered as far as his private and family life are concerned, his relationship with the believers and non-believers, and his ability to learn and to teach.

Shepherding Towards Christ

He then provided us with a simplified portrait of the shepherding guidelines that a bishop should present to every category of his flock, to experience life with the Lord Jesus Christ through their daily behaviour. By that, he seeks from the shepherds to provide their flock, not with solid laws and hard statutes, but to proclaim Christianity as a life together with Jesus Christ, testable by both the elder and child, lived by both man and woman, and well received by both the master and the servant. In short, every believer would find comfort in the Lord Jesus Christ, through his daily life.

Living with Christ in our Daily Behaviour

Finally, the apostle demonstrates to us how to live with the Lord Christ in our behaviour with other, a believer should not lead a blind, bigoted life, nor create for himself an independent and an isolated society within the society, or shut himself in. He should readily submit to rulers and governing authorities with joy and gladness of heart, as to the Lord, and he should love everyone and open his heart wide to all, without flattering nor showing partiality at the expense of the truth.

Introduction to
THE EPISTLE TO
PHILEMON

INTRODUCTION AND HISTORY

This epistle, which consists of only one chapter, has such strong and beautiful statements that are considered to be a gem in the Holy Bible. It reveals the real fatherhood of the ministers of Christ, Christian love, and forgiveness. It demonstrates the power of the gospel in winning over a runaway thief and salve, and in changing his master's mind. It reveals the faith that works by love.

AUDIENCE OF THE EPISTLE

Who is Philemon?

Philemon was a member of the Church of Colossae who later became a bishop. He seemed to have held its assemblies in his house (v. 2). Philemon's benevolence (v. 5-7) and St. Paul's request for him to prepare a lodging (v. 22), indicate that he was a man of some means.

St. Paul had never been in Colossae (Col. 2: 1) and so Philemon must have met him elsewhere, possibly in Ephesus, which was not far away. Some scholars believe that, though not recorded, St. Paul visited Colossae during his three-year stay at Ephesus (Acts). It would seem that Philemon owed his conversion to St. Paul (v. 19).

AUTHOR OF THE EPISTLE

The Author of the Epistle

This epistle is a personal letter of intercession written by St. Paul, probably from Rome, to Philemon at Colossae in Asia Minor (Col 4:7-9). It was written near the end of St. Paul's first Roman imprisonment--at the same time as Ephesians and Colossians.

PURPOSE OF THE EPISTLE TO PHILEMON

The Aim of the Epistle

St. Paul wished to save the runaway slave from the severe and cruel punishment he deserved according to Roman law, which gave the runaway slave no rights of life or liberty.

MAIN THEMES AND STRUCTURE
OF THE EPISTLE TO PHILEMON

This epistle shows St. Paul as an example of the following

1. St. Paul showed pastoral or fatherly love towards everybody, especially the lowly. He would take care of everyone, even the runaway slave, as if it were his only son.

2. Wisdom in dealing with Philemon who was injured by his runaway slave, Onesimus. At the same time, St. Paul realised that the Christian brotherhood obliterated all social and class distinctions.

3. Regarding the duty of obedience to the law on the part of converts, Onesimus must return to his master.

4. Using the abilities and gifts of every member of the Church, St. Paul noticed that the converted slave was very gifted, could serve Christ (v 17, 18) and work for the edification of the Church. Onesimus helped the apostle Paul and then was ordained bishop, taking care of Christ's people.

5. Interceding for others, St. Paul's intercession for Onesimus breathes the unique propitious intercession of Christ for His own before the Father. St. Paul asked Philemon to receive Onesimus as if he were Paul himself, and to put any demerit on his account. Our Lord Jesus Christ is our representative before the Father; all our sins are reckoned or imputed to His account.

Introduction to
THE EPISTLE TO
THE HEBREWS

INTRODUCTION AND HISTORY

St. Paul was called to minister to the Gentiles; however, he was not prevented from serving his own people, especially those who were living among the Gentiles. He wished to be accursed from Christ for their sake (Romans 9:3). God did not prevent him from serving them, but he sent him for a specific mission, to serve the Gentiles. As he said that the Lord Christ did not send him to baptise (1 Corinthians 1:17), but this does not mean that he is not allowed to baptise. His love for everyone made him concerned about all groups of people; thus, he did not shun writing to this group of people when he realised their need, especially because he is superior to others in studying Moses' Law and the Jewish rites.

AUDIENCE OF THE EPISTLE

The epistle was written to the Jews who were unable to separate themselves from the Jewish tradition as they accepted their faith in Jesus Christ, and to help the Gentiles so they are not confused on the practices of the faith now that Christ has risen.

Place of Writing:

St. John Chrysostom said that St. Paul wrote it in Jerusalem and Palestine.

AUTHOR OF THE EPISTLE

The Author of the Epistle

Since the name of the writer is not mentioned in the book, the early theologians have since disagreed about who wrote it. In the West, Tertullian, one of the second century scholars, mentioned that Barnabas wrote it. However, by comparing it to the epistle of Barnabas, we find that there is a vast difference, which ascertains that it is impossible to have one write for both. Another thought prevailed in the West that St. Clement of Rome is the writer. However, after the fourth century, it was agreed that St Paul was the writer.

In the East, it was mostly agreed from the beginning that St. Paul was the writer. In general, this was what the Eastern Church has accepted, specifically the school of Alexandria. Eusebius mentioned that St. Clement of Alexandria had a missing piece of work, where it occurred that his philosophy professor, Pantentius, referred to the epistle and to St. Paul as its writer.

We can summarise the view of the theologians concerning who wrote the epistle through the following points:

1. The writer is St. Paul: this thought prevailed in the Eastern Church since its beginning, then settled in the Western Church. Some of those who mentioned this view are St. Pantenius, St. John Chrysostom, St.

Augustine. This remains the prevailing view among the majority of theologians

2. Barnabas: Tertullian, Weisler and Ulmann

3. Luke, the evangelist: Origen mentioned this opinion, Ebrabd, and Calvin accepted it

4. Clement of Rome: an early Western view which disappeared completely, however, a minority accepted it like Reithmuier Erasmus

5. Silas: Rohme, Mynster

6. Apollos: Luthea, Semler

Why didn't St. Paul mention his name?

St. Paul usually mentions his name in the beginning of his epistle, so why didn't he mention his name in this epistle? St. Paul was known in the early Church to be the apostle for the Gentiles, whilst St. Peter, St. John, St. James and others were apostles for the Jews. Thus, St. Paul was more liberal in matters pertaining to some Jewish rituals, which made many Christians, who were from Hebrew origin, dislike him.

It was mentioned about him that, "…they have been informed about you that you teach all the Jews who are among the Gentiles to forsake Moses…" (Acts 21:21). Since this epistle was directed to the Hebrew Christians, it was appropriate to not mention his name lest they not read it.

PURPOSE OF THE EPISTLE TO THE HEBREWS

The Aim of the Epistle:

We can realise the purpose of this epistle when we know the true picture of the early Church. The apostles together with the Jews who were converted, used to worship in the temple to follow the law and adhere themselves to the Jewish nation and its hope, but in new spiritual hope through Christ Jesus. Truly, many of them were unable to separate themselves from this nation, not realising that the concept of the Church as one body of Christ contains the Jew as well as the Gentile, without partiality. The Lord and the servant are equal, male and female are the same, without any preference. Therefore, if the Church is persecuted and the Sanhedrin condemned the Hebrew Christians by expelling them from the holy places, because they are defiled and considered unbelievers against the Law, then they are deeply hurt. They felt that for the sake of the Messiah, they were isolated from God's old people who were waiting for the Messiah. This was a difficult trial for them and a deep wound which tremendously hurt them. They were expelled from the household and citizenship of Israel and from the temple. Thus, the apostle writes to them to confirm that they gained more than what they had lost. Hence, the world "for us" was repeated several times. They obtained the true heavenly temple instead of the symbolic temple, and they got the heavenly high priest instead of the Levitical priesthood. They were related to the church of the firstborn, the celebration of angels, instead of the Jewish citizenship, and the heavenly Jerusalem instead of the earthly Jerusalem. The purpose of this epistle was to confirm that Christianity is not deprivation, but rather it is obtaining the heavenly matters and enjoying eternity. Truly, it is expelling outside of the camp with the crucified Christ outside Jerusalem, but in the meantime, it is enjoyment of His city, the city of the Heavenly Firstborn.

The camp was the favourite place of the Jews, but the Lord Christ was raised on the cross outside it, so that His Church may go out to Him, as expelled from the Jewish nation – bearing the literal thinking – sharing with Him His suffering and shame.

Since the Jewish temple was about to be totally demolished in Jerusalem, along with all the Jewish rites, sacrifices, and the Levitical priesthood, the Apostle revealed the Christian temple, the Sacrifice of Christ, and the new priesthood. He clarified the reality of the old shadows, its power and integrity, and that they all go back to its deep roots in the Lord Jesus Christ, the Eternal Sacrifice and Priest.

MAIN THEMES AND STRUCTURE OF THE EPISTLE TO THE HEBREWS

SPECIAL FEATURES OF THE EPISTLE

The Old Testament through Christian Eyes

This epistle is considered to be an epistle to the Romans and was written in a way with lots of proof. It is specifically characterised among the other books of the New Testament by its teachings and proofs being based on the well-known books of the Old Testament, which is familiar to the Jewish people. In it, you find that the Old Testament bears the anointing of Christianity, offering new perspectives to the Old Testament by the Sacrifice of the Cross. St. Paul presented a heavenly song in an excellent style, through the inspiration of the Holy Spirit. The purpose is to withdraw the heart of the Christian Hebrew from shadow to the truth, from outward physical worship, to Christ's supreme service. This epistle is like a beautiful symphony revealing the unity of the two Testaments, through the manifestation of the hidden truth behind the Law and the true sacrifice.

Circumcision

The apostle handled the issues of the Jewish regulations and the Law, like circumcision, as he did in other epistles--just like the ones to the Galatians and the Colossians, noting that these were private matters which one could reject or accept. However, in this epistle, he writes about a topic which involves the whole community, pertaining to the Jewish temple which was closed before everyone and the Jewish citizenship of which they were involuntarily deprived of.

Practical Commandments

The apostle devoted the last two chapters, as he always used to in other epistles, to the practical commandments, like commitment to love, obedience, and strife. But throughout the entirety of the epistle, he weaved in practical applications to transform the dogma to an experienced life. He wrote not to fulfill one's thoughts theoretically, but to satisfy one's inner depths, feelings, as well as behaviour. Thus, one's life can be absolutely made new in the Lord

Different to the Rest

This epistle was different from the rest of St Paul's epistles, with the major topics that usually occupy his mind, he did not write about. In this epistle, he did not write about the Church as the body of Christ, whose Head is the Lord, nor about our unity with the Father in His Son through the Holy Spirit, nor about our fellowship with the saviour sharing His suffering then His glories. Instead, he wrote about a unique topic, which is the deprivation of the Hebrew Christian from the temple and the rituals. Simultaneously, he concentrates on the priesthood of Christ, who intercedes with His blood in front of His Father until we enjoy the heavenly temple and the angelic rite, through our unity in Him.

Introduction to
THE CATHOLIC EPISTLES

IN THE INTRODUCTION TO
THE CATHOLIC EPISTLES, YOU WILL FIND

About the author

✳

Audience of the Epistle

✳

Purpose of the Epistle

✳

Main themes and structure of the Epistle

THE CATHOLIC LETTERS

The Church calls the seven epistles (James, First and Second Peter, First, Second and Third letters of John and also Jude) the Catholic letters, that is universal because they are general, that is, they were not directed toward a certain Church nor a city nor a specific person, as in the case of the apostle's letters.

Although the second and third epistles of St. John was addressed to two specific people, because they were too short, they were just considered as an extension to the first epistle, especially because they have the same characteristics and style. There are similarities across the epistles, specifically between First Peter and St. James, Second Peter and Jude, and the three epistles of St. John.

The Church gives special attention to these epistles, and so it requires us to read parts of them on most occasions, especially during the prayers of the liturgies. St. Jerome said that these epistles were characterised by being written in great detail, but also concisely. Being detailed in meaning and concise in expressions made them difficult to be properly understood.

Introduction to

THE EPISTLE OF ST. JAMES

THE AUTHOR OF THE EPISTLE

In the New Testament there were three people called James:

1) James the son of Zebedee (Matthew 10:2):

He was one of the twelve disciples and the brother of John the evangelist. He cannot be the writer of the epistle because Herod Agrippa I murdered him in the year 44 A.D. (Acts 12:1). At that time, the Christian Churches were not established yet to allow for some of the disciples to send epistles, and the dispersion had not yet occurred, nor had the heresies had appeared.

2) James the son of Alphaeus (Matthew 10:3):

There is a lot of research to assess whether he is the same one as James the brother of the Lord or a different one.

3) James the brother or the Lord (Galatians 1:19):

This James is his cousin. Everyone agrees that he is the writer of the epistle. Here is a summary of his biography:

Some believe that he was not James the son of Alphaeus, one of the twelve apostles, and the brother of Joses, Judas and Simon. Therefore, he was not a believer during the life of the Lord Jesus on earth, as the evangelist said, "For even His brothers did not believe in Him" (John 7:5). But after the resurrection, he believed in the Lord Jesus, as it is written in the book of Acts, "They all continued with one accord in prayer and supplication, with the women and Mary the mother of Jesus, and with His brothers" (Acts 1:14), the disciples were gathered with the brothers of the Lord Jesus.

St Jerome mentioned, as well as history has confirmed, that St. James was ordained a bishop of Jerusalem and stayed in it until the day of his martyrdom. He wrote a liturgy, which the Armenians still use up until now.

St. Epiphanius and Eusebius said that he was a Nazarene for the Lord, since he was in his mother's womb, so he did not drink any wine nor any intoxicating drink, never shaved his head and always ate beans.

He was called James the Righteous, because he loved worship and from the abundance of his kneeling for prayer, his knees were like the knees of a camel. St. Jerome mentioned that the Jews greatly feared him and hastened to touch his clothes. One time, they brought him to the top of the temple to witness against Christ, so he told them, "Christ now is sitting in the highest at the right hand of the Father, and He will judge these people." When they heard him, some screamed, "Hosanna to the Son of David." The scribes and Pharisees attacked him while saying, "The righteous has strayed." Then they threw him from the top to bottom. After falling, he knelt on his knees asking for forgiveness for them, but they hastened and stoned him. Then a man came and struck him with a hammer on his head. Instantly, he was martyred in around the year 62 A.D. and was buried at the place of his martyrdom close to the Temple. Josephus the historian, said that one of the reasons for the destruction of Jerusalem was that its people had killed James the righteous, so God's wrath came upon them.

In the year 52 A.D. he presided over the first ecumenical council in Jerusalem to discuss the faith of the Gentiles. St. James issued the resolution of the council (Acts 15). The apostle called him one of the pillars of the Church, and he mentioned his name before St. Peter and St. John (Galatians 2:9).

The Epistle's Agreement with the personality of St. James as it was in the New Testament

When we first became acquainted with James, we found him to be an unbeliever of the Lord Jesus (Mk 3:21, John 7:5), but he also wasn't considered a stranger, for he had great love and respect for the person of the Lord. However, maybe he could not agree with Jesus' method, as he had no understanding of the significance of His mission yet. It was the Lord's resurrection that caused the change in his mind, for not only do we find him among the Lord's disciples (Acts 1:14), but James was mentioned when talking about the resurrection apparitions (1 Cor 15:7). St. Paul likely mentioned him because St. James told him about it (Gal 1:19). It is significant that Paul counts him among the Pillars of the Jerusalem Church, and in Acts 15, we see him as the head of the church council of Jerusalem.

All of this agrees with the personality of St. James, the writer of the epistle--a famous person of Jewish origin, who is keen to keep the law as he writes in Jerusalem to the Christian congregation of Jewish origin.

Objections to the Author of the Epistle

Some modern critics protested against St. James being the writer of the epistle, saying that the rich and elevated Greek language of the epistle reveals it is no way that the writer can be a simple Galilean person. They explain this through the divine work, i.e. the "inspiration of the Holy Spirit" that the modern scholars neglect. There is no evidence that denies St. James being instructed with the Greek culture, particularly that this area was abounding in Greek cities. However, the Mediterranean Sea Jews were known to be trained in Greek culture (Helenian) on the highest level. The proof of this is their role in translating the Old Testament, the Septuagint translation

The second objection is that if the writer is James, then he would have pointed out that he is the Lord's brother to give more importance and value to the epistle. The reply to this is that this objection is not accepted, firstly because the Saint realising how the highly esteemed, Jesus Chris, considered himself as a "slave" and "servant" (1:1). Besides, the Lord Jesus Christ does not reply on the basis of mere bodily acquaintance (2 Cor, 5:16) or blood relationship.

Some doubt about the writer, saying that if the writer was James, the Lord's brother, then he would have recorded the great events of our Lord's life, such as his death and resurrection, especially that when he met Paul, he discussed the matter. The reply for this is that James himself in his speech, which is mentioned in the Book of Acts (chapter 15), didn't point out such matters. This was because firstly, he had a certain aim, which was not a display of the events of the Lord's life or His theological thoughts. Secondly, because these events were quite well known in the Church and did not need to be recorded, particularly that the purpose of his writings is merely precise Christian behaviour.

Other critics say that if the writer was St. James the brother of the Lord, then he would have written about the law differently, as some scholars think. As an example, we find dealing with the problem of circumcision and Jewish rites surpassing that of the behaviour aspect. The reply to this is that St. James most probably wrote the epistle before the meeting of the assembly mentioned in the Book of Acts (Ch. 15). However, being the one responsible of the Church of Jerusalem representing the Church of Jewish origin he refrained from interfering in such a dispute.

It especially seems that he is inclined to be nice to the Jews at first, not because he is convinced of the importance of circumcision and other matters, but to gain their side and not to stumble thousands of them. Thus, he had his role of the purification of Paul and his entry into the temple according to the Jewish rites so as to not stumble them (Acts 21:17-26). We notice that once people came from James to St. Peter, the saint separated himself from the Gentiles in fear of the circumcised

(Gal 2:11,12). This matter aroused St. Paul who resisted and confronted him.

THE AUDIENCE OF THE EPISTLE

Who was this Epistle Written To?

It was written to the twelve tribes in the dispersion. There were many opinions to interpret this, however, which are mentioned below:

1. Some believe that it was written to those who were previously Jews and were dispersed before Christianity. God has used that dispersion in preaching Christianity, and so some believed when they went to Jerusalem on the day of Pentecost. Those who were originally Jews and believed in Christ, became the subject of persecution from their brothers, the Jews who had rejected believing in the Lord Jesus.

2. Others believe that the Jews, seeing that some believed in Christ, and because they were waiting for a Messiah who gives them earthly authority and submits other kingdoms under their domain (unfortunately the Zionist ideas is still in the minds of the Jews), stirred the Romans against the Christians. That is why the Christians sought the Gentiles, for they found in them a wide welcome, more so than the Jews.

3. Some believe that mentioning the twelve tribes does not mean that they were of Jewish origin, but that it refers to the Church, no matter who are her members, is the heir to the tribes spiritually. The attribute "Israel" has been denied from the Jews. Therefore, we do not believe that the Jews are the new Israel. although they assume that, for they have denied faith and were denied being called "God's people."

Writing to Jerusalem before its Destruction

The conditions of the community to whom were witnesses to St. James, was during the period before the fall of Jerusalem. We find him talking about the rich who press on the poor (5:1-6). This fits the period that precedes the destruction and not that follows it. As well as this, the mention of wars and fights between them suits the condition of Jerusalem before its destruction. There is also the absence of any allusion to master and slaves, and by the omission of any denunciation of idolatry, all of which fits a Christian of Jewish origin that lives as a sanctified person to the Lord, in the period preceding the destruction of Jerusalem

Time and Place or Writing

It was written during the time when the Jews were persecuting the Church for their rich people, and chiefs stirred the persecution (Acts 4:1, 5:17). This was before the persecution of Domitian and Trajan. It was written before the fall of Jerusalem, that is, before the dispersion of the Jews (68 A.D.). Some believe that it was written around 60 A.D. or 61 A.D., during the time when all the heresies mentioned in the epistle were spread.

THE PURPOSE OF THE EPISTLE
OF ST. JAMES

The Aim of the Epistle

1. To encourage Christians to endure tribulation when they suffer from the Jews and to explain the meaning of temptation on the light of the suffering Lord

2. To encourage them to be steadfast in faith, the practical faith

3. To clarify the concept of living faith and its correlation with deeds

4. To reveal dangers of some sins, which some may have thought them to be trivial.

MAIN THEMES AND STRUCTURE
OF THE EPISTLE OF ST. JAMES

Special Features of this Epistle

1. It adopted the practical style regarding the holiness of the Christian life

2. Its expressions are easy, clear, and richly depicted in brief. It was Palestine that inspired the apostle here with many similes (1:11; 3:11,12; 5:7, 17, 18)

3. It was strict in rebuking with an overflow of love and compassion

4. It is similar to the "Sermon on the Mount," from the points of the many practical commandments, to the extent that some thought it is a gathering of the words of the Lord Jesus Christ. Both have mentioned the spiritual outlook of the Law in its depth, about the fatherhood of God and choosing between the love of God and the love of the world.

5. It is similar in many of its expressions with the book of Joshua, the son of Sirach and the book if Wisdom and the first epistle of St. Peter

6. It is related to the Old Testament, for in mentioning patience, the writer referred to Job (James 5) and in mentioning prayer, he referred to Elijah. However, it is characterised by the nature of the New Testament. He repeated the word "brothers" and "the new birth" (1:18), the perfect Law, the Law of liberty (1:25) and the sacraments of the Church (James 5).

ARE THERE CONTRADICTIONS
BETWEEN THE EPISTLE AND ST. PAUL'S EPISTLE?

Due to the superficiality in understanding the word of God, some thought that there is contradiction between what is mentioned in this epistle and what is mentioned in the epistles of St. Paul, especially the epistle to the Romans. They believe that St. James did not care about faith and that St. Paul does not care about deeds. However, when we study these epistles, we notice the following:

1. There is no contradiction in thoughts between the two epistles, especially that both agreed together in the first ecumenical council, which was presided by St. James (Acts 15)

2. St. James addresses some believers who deviated from abiding in the light, claiming that faith only can justify them and there is no need for deeds. However, St. Paul, as an apostle to the Gentiles, confronted people who were originally Jews and were calling for every Gentile to adopt Judaism and undergo circumcision. They depended on the works of the Jewish rites, in itself claiming that keeping such things must justify the person. Moreover, those who were originally Gentiles depended on their works before the faith to justify them. Therefore, no wonder, if St. James has concentrated on the works of the apostle on faith, rejecting anyone to depend on the Jewish rites and self righteous works.

3. St. Paul and St. James agree about the importance of justification by works. But what works? Works, which are based on the worthiness of the blood of Christ, and not self-righteous works. St. Paul confirms that by saying, "If I have all the faith to move mountains but have no love, it profits me nothing." (1 Cor 13:2). Faith without love is nothing and cannot justify, what is love as St Paul explained in the same chapter except practical love, "love is patient and kind, does not envy..." No wonder if the apostle, who concentrated on faith, now confirms that love is greater than faith (1 Cor 13:13).

4. St. Paul does not stop at the importance of works, but emphasises that evil works destroy man, even if he were a believer.

5. St. James does not ignore faith (James 1:6; 5:15), but on the contrary, he connects works with faith and faith with works, without separation or discrimination.

CANONISATION OF THE EPISTLE

The epistle of St James suffered much in the 16th century, for it concentrates on the good deeds. Martin Luther described it as an epistle of straw. This view differs from that of the early Church, which understood it within the context of the whole scripture. Without it, the grasp of ethical Christianity is incomplete. Among the evidence for its canonisation are:

First: The External Evidence

In the second century, Origen pointed to it as an epistle of St. James. He knew it as a canonical book. There are many quotations of it in the writings of St. Clement of Rome, the Didache, the epistle of Barnabas, St. Ignatius of Antioch, Hermas etc.

Some scholars believe that this epistle did not spread at the same rate of St. Paul's epistles, especially in the West, because it was written to the Christians of Jewish origin in the East, and it was not addressed to those of a Gentiles origin.

It's to be noted that there is no mention of this epistle in the Muratorian Canon, which also makes no mention of the Hebrews and the Petrine epistles. However, this may be due to the obviously corrupt state of the text of that Canon.

Second: The External Evidence

The writer introduces himself quite simply as "James, a servant of God and of the Lord Jesus Christ" (1:1). This simple description reveals that the writer is quite famous, and since two are well known by that name, one of which is easily narrowed down to one. James, the son of Zebedee who was martyred by the hand of Herod in 44 A.D. and the other James the Lord's brother, who had his vital role in the early Church. Thus, it is obvious that he, by the inspiration of the Holy Spirit, is the writer of the epistle.

The following evidences declare the genuineness of the epistle and that St. James is actually the writer of the epistle:

The Author's Jewish Background

No one can deny that the author's mind has drawn much from the Old Testament. Besides the direct quotations (1:11; 2:28, 11, 23; 4:6), there are indirect and innumerable allusions to the Old Testament (1:10-2:21, 23, 25; 3:9; 4:6; 5:2, 11, 17, 18 etc.). When the writer required illustrations for prayer and patience, he turned to the Old Testament characters. He also concentrated on keeping the Law (2:9, 11). There are many other obvious indicators of Jewish mind. Certain other terms such as, "Lord of Sabaoth" (5:4) "assembly" (2:2) "Father Abraham" (2:21) also show this.

Similarities between James' Epistle and St. James' speech in the book of Acts (Ch. 15):

As his use of the word "brothers" (2:15/ Acts 15:13); "greetings" (1:1/ Acts 15:23) also the honourable name by which you are called 2:7/Acts 15:17…plus may other parallels that were found there.

Similarities between the Epistle and The Gospels:

Many scholars think that there is a strong similarity between what came in the epistle and the teachings of Lord Jesus Christ. We can see these similarities through the following examples:

- (1:2) Joy in the midst of trial (Mt 5:10-12)
- (1:4) Exhortation to perfection (Mt 5:48)
- (1:5) Asking for good gifts (Mt 7:7 etc.)
- (1:20) Anger (Mt 5:22)
- (1:22) About the heavens and doers of the word (Mt 7:24 etc.)
- (2:10) The whole law to be kept (Mt 5:9)
- (2:13) Blessing of mercifulness (Mt 5:7)
- (3:18) Blessing of peacemaker (Mt 5:9)

• (4:4) Loving the world as an enmity against God (Mt 6:24)

• (4:10) Blessing of humility (Mt 5:5)

• (4:11,12) Condemnation (Mt 7:1-5)

• (5:2) Moth rust spoiling riches (Mt 6:19)

• (5:10) The prophets as our examples (Mt 5:12)

• (5:12) Oaths (Mt 5:33-37)

In addition to these parallels, there are others between what came in this epistle and the teachings of the Lord Jesus Christ in different parts, such as:

• (1:6) Exercise of faith without doubting (Mt 21:21)

• (2:8) Great is the commandment of loving the neighbour (Mt 22:39)

• (3:1) On the desire to be called teacher (Mt 23:8-12)

• (3:2) On the dangers of hasty speech (Mt 12:36-37)

• (4:9) The divine judge at the doors (Mt 24:33)

Introduction to
THE FIRST EPISTLE
OF ST. PETER

THE AUTHOR OF THE EPISTLE

The Writer of the Epistle

The scholars and the fathers of the Church have unanimously agreed that St. Peter was the writer of this epistle. St. Ireneaus was the first to use excerpts from the epistle mentioning St. Peter's name, however, we find similar excerpts in the writings of many fathers that followed St. Ireneaus, such as the epistle of St. Barnabas, the writings of St. Clement of Rome, the book of the Shepherd by Hermas, and the writings of St. Polycarp the Martyr. St. Clement of Alexandria, Tertullian, Eusebius of Caesarea have also mentioned that the epistle of St. Peter is widely accepted by the Church. The epistle is in harmony with the style of St. Peter's sermons, as mentioned in the book of Acts. For example:

Firstly, he referred to God as Judge, who judges with no partiality (Chapter 1:7 compared with Acts 10:34).

Secondly, he emphasised the Father who raised Jesus Christ from the dead (Chapter 1:21 compared with Acts 2:32 & 3:15, 10:40).

Thirdly, his declaration that the Lord Jesus is the chief cornerstone (Chapter 2:7 compared with Acts 4:11)

St. Peter did not know the Greek language; however, S.t Mark and St. Selvanus were fluent, and they were very close to St. Peter.

THE AUDIENCE OF THE EPISTLE

Who was the Epistle Written to?

It was written to the pilgrim of the Dispersion in Pontus, Galatia, Cappadocia, Asia and Bithynia in Asia Minor (Ch. 1:1). Some believe that it was not St Peter's intention to organise the regions by their official geographical locations, for example: Pontus was in the district of Galatia until the year 63 A.D. and Phrygia, which occupies a large area in Asia Minor, was not mentioned. However, the carrier of the epistle could not have passed from Cappadocia to Asia without passing through Phrygia. Thus, it would have been impossible not to enter the region of Phrygia to reach the many intended readers of this epistle (Acts 18:23). Therefore, these names meant all of Asia Minor.

On the day of Pentecost, there were some from Cappadocia, Pontus and Asia (Acts 2:9). Pontus is located by "Bohrof El Karm", which is the origin of Aquila. Since St. Peter started addressing his epistle to this district, Tertullian, St. Cyprian the Martyr, St. Cyprian the Martyr, and St. Jerome called this epistle "the epistle to Pontus." The district of Asia under Asia Minor this was the place where Aquila was born (Acts 18:2), and Bithynia, which from Constantinople was near Pontus.

Time and Place of Writing:

• It was written between the years 63 and 67 A.D. during the persecution of Nero (54-68 A.D).

• It was written from Babylon (Ch. 5:13). There were different opinions regarding the city of Babylon. All agreed that it was not the Babylon on the Euphrates River, for it had been destroyed by that time. Tradition does not mention that St. Peter had gone there and it was very unlikely that St. Mark and Silas had gone there in their travels

• Catholics claim that Babylon refers to Rome, relying on the fact that Babel, mentioned in the Book of Revelation, refers to Rome. However, there is nothing that either supports or refutes this opinion:

 Firstly, why did St. Peter not mention the name Rome?

Secondly, historically, St. Peter did not arrive in Rome early enough before his martyrdom to allow him to write two epistles

Thirdly, arranging the provinces as mentioned in the epistle from East to West supports the idea that the epistle was written somewhere in the East.

Finally, the most likely option is that Babylon is Old Cairo, which was inhabited by a Jewish community and was a station for Roman Soldiers. Historical traditions which state that St Mark came to Egypt in the year 61 A.D. or 62 A.D., support this opinion.

PURPOSE OF THE FIRST EPISTLE OF PETER

Aim of the Epistle

The purpose of this epistle is to encourage the believers to accept suffering. This epistle is considered to be an excellent source of comfort, and every chapter is filled with a comforting message. It also was written to reveal the practical, holy mutual relationships in the family, society and the Church through faith in the crucified Lord Jesus.

MAIN THEMES AND STRUCTURE
OF THE FIRST EPISTLE OF PETER

Special Features of the Epistle

It is very similar to some of St. Paul's epistles, especially Ephesians, Romans, Galatians and Titus. We also find many similarities between this epistle and St. Paul's to the Hebrews. Because he is the apostle to the Jews, the apostle of circumcision, St. Peter took many excerpts from the Old Testament. St. Peter often refers to the words of the Lord Jesus because he was an eyewitness to what the Lord Jesus said and did.

Introduction to
THE SECOND
EPISTLE OF ST. PETER

THE AUTHOR OF THE EPISTLE

Many doubted the writer of this epistle. St. Eronemos said that there are a few who doubted who the writer of the second epistle is due to the difference in style between it and the first one. However, he ascertained that St. Peter is the one who wrote it, and considered it one of the Catholicon epistles in his letter to Paulimius. He clarified that the differences between the two epistles is the difference in translation. The following are the proofs that the author is St Peter:

First: some writers tried to count the number of common Greek words between the two epistles and they found that 369 words were used in the first epistle and not the second, and that 230 words were used in the second epistle and not the first, and that 100 words were used across the two epistles.

We notice that one sixth of the common words between the two epistles is a big percentage to make us not doubt. Moreover, St. Peter does not know the Greek language, so the one who translated the first epistle for him is different from the one who translated the second epistle. Also, the difference in the subject and the purpose, lessens the existence of common words

Second: the early Church accepted that epistle, for Yusabius the historian mentioned that St. Clement of Alexandria excerpted some parts from it. St. Jerome, Firmilians, the bishop of Caesarea and Origen his disciple, have also ascertained that St. Peter is the writer

St. Clement of Rome excerpted many of his writings from it. There were many words and expressions only mentioned in the writings of this epistle, such as the road of truth, not being diligent and unfruitful, eternal kingdom, and the prophetic words. This epistle is very similar to the epistle of St. Jude.

Third: St. Peter mentioned the epistles of St. Paul in chapters 3, 5 and 16, which made some think that it was written at a later date, after St. Paul's letters

To refute that, the epistles were written and spread between the different churches immediately (Col 4:16), besides having a strong friendship between the two apostles, which made St. Peter know St. Paul's letters

Fourth: the testimony of the writer himself, as we see in the following ways:

1. He started the epistle by saying "Simon Peter"

2. He called himself one among the apostles (1:1, 3:2)

3. He was with the Lord himself in the transfiguration (1:16-18)

4. He wrote that he was writing a previous epistle (3:1)

THE AUDIENCE OF THE EPISTLE

Who was this Epistle Written For?

It was directed to the Christians of Asia Minor, of which the first epistle was directed to. He wrote, "I now write to you this second epistle..." (2 Pet 3:1)

Time of Writing

It was written toward the end of his life, as it is apparent from him saying, "Knowing that shortly I must put off my tent..." (2 Pet 1:14), that is between the years 64 and 68 A.D.

THE PURPOSE OF THE SECOND EPISTLE OF ST. PETER

The Aim of the Epistle

Since the Lord has declared to him his departure from this world, he wanted to send his children his final commandment to tell them about the precious yearning of his heart which is, "The kingdom of heaven and the second coming of the Lord." Waiting for the heavenly kingdom drives the believer to the life of holiness and rejecting heresies.

MAIN THEMES AND STRUCTURE OF THE SECOND EPISTLE OF ST. PETER

Similarities between this Epistle and the Epistle of St. Jude

The two epistles are very similar, especially with what was written in the second chapter:

• False teachers (2 Pet 2:1-3) (Jude v.4)

• Destruction of the angels who sinned (2 Pet 2:4) (Jude v.6)

• Destruction of Sodom and Gomorrah (2 Pet 2:2) (Jude v.7)

• Uncleanness and speaking of evil dignitaries (2 Pet 2:10-12) (Jude v.8-10)

• Feasting of the teachers (2 Pet 2:13) (Jude v.12)

• Following the way of Balaam (2 Pet 2:15) (Jude v.11)

• Reserving the heretics for darkness (2 Pet 2:17) (Jude v.13)

• Speaking swelling words of emptiness (2 Pet 2:18) (Jude v. 16)

• Reminding them of the apostles' sayings (2 Pet 3:1-3) (Jude v. 17,18)

This close resemblance between the two epistles in meaning, purpose, style, and even words, made some scholars assume the following:

1. That one of them depended on the other, for some said that St. Peter depended on St. Jude's letter while claim the opposite

2. Some said that the second chapter of the second epistle of St. Peter until the second verse of the third chapter, were added to the original letter depending on the letter of St. Jude, and that the rest of the epistle is its true content. No one supported this point of view, however, for moving to this part (2 Pet 2:1-3) is a natural transition and if we omit it, the epistle would not be complete. Moreover, the unity of the style in this epistle proves that this assumption is false

3. Many of the expressions in the epistle of St. Jude clarified what was mentioned in the second epistle of St. Peter. However, St. Peter used future tense, while St. Jude mentioned it as a true event, which is how the epistle of St. Peter preceded the epistle of St. Jude. It was mentioned in the epistle of St. Jude that the apostles have prophesied about these matters (Jude 17,18). It is likely the case that he meant St. Peter as one of them. St. Jude used some expressions in the same way of St. Paul, which St. Peter did not use (like to those who are called), the saints (Jude v.3), the dreamers (Jude v.8). These made some say that St. Jude

did not excerpt his epistle from St. Peter, but that the similarities are due to the unity of circumstances, unity of purpose and unity of time.

Introduction to
THE FIRST
EPISTLE OF ST. JOHN

THE AUTHOR OF THE EPISTLE

The early Church agrees that the writer is St. John the beloved disciple. It corresponds with his gospel in many expressions, as well as in theological thought. St. John briefly mentions the things he wrote in his gospel, assuming that the reader has already read his gospel. St. John did not mention his name, nor did he start with an introduction, or conclude with special peace. However, the epistle was written in the style of a letter directed from a dignified father to his beloved children, who are related in strong spiritual bond. As such, we can think of this epistle as a pastoral pamphlet directed to all Christians.

THE AUDIENCE OF THE EPISTLE

Circumstances under which the epistle was written

Towards the end of the first century and the beginning of the second century, some heresies appeared which pertain to the person of the

Lord Jesus. These heresies are based on the existence of two Gods; one for God who created the spirit, and the other for who founded material, which is evil, and God cannot create evil. Therefore, because God cannot come as real flesh, for the flesh is evil, He appeared to people as if He was hungry and thirsty, so He ate and drank, and He was crucified and died. This pagan thought defiles man's outlook of the flesh and material matters. Therefore, the early Church confirmed the Christian understanding of the flesh and material being, noting that they are good because God creates them, however, it is man who defiles them by his evil. This idea mars the love of God who resembled us in everything except sin, and it contradicts the scriptures and destroys the essence of the redemption, which is based on our salvation by the blood of Christ shed on the cross.

Time and Place of Writing

This epistle was written in Ephesus towards the end of the first century, after the destruction of the temple and the Jewish nation ended. That is why St. John does not mention the persecutions that the Jews have stirred against the Christians, but instead wrote about the attack of some heretics.

PURPOSE OF THE FIRST EPISTLE
OF ST. JOHN

Aim of the Epistle

St. John mentions four goals in this epistle:

1. That our joy may be full (1 John 1:4)

2. That we do not sin (1 John 2:1)

3. To avoid the deceivers (1 John 2:26)

4. To know that we have eternal life and to have confidence in Him (1 John 5:13,14)

MAIN THEMES AND STRUCTURE
OF THE EPISTLES OF ST. JOHN

The early Church gave credit to St. John the beloved, the disciple of our Lord Jesus Christ, to writing the three epistles. We notice that there are similarities between these epistles

Similarities between the first two Epistles

1. The purpose of their writing: that our joy may be full (1 John 1:4; 2 John 12)

2. They focus on the commandment of "love," which should be translated to practical behaviour in our lives as children of God.

3. This practical behaviour, which accompanies the right faith, distinguishes God's children who are steadfast in the faith and Satan's children who are living in darkness and who reject the Son of God, whether by faith or rejecting His work in our practical life

Similarities between the second and third epistles

We can see similarities between their styles by comparing the following verses:

1. The second epistle verse 1 with the third epistle verse 3

2. The second epistle verse 4 with the third epistle verses 3,4

3. The second epistle verse 12 with the third epistle verses 3,14

Introduction to
THE SECOND
EPISTLE OF ST. JOHN

THE AUTHOR OF THE EPISTLE

St. John the beloved wrote this epistle and the one following it. He wrote them while he was in Ephesus. If he had written them on the island of Patmos, he would have referred to what he had seen there.

AUDIENCE OF THE EPISTLE

Who was this Epistle written to?

This is the only book in the Bible directed to a lady for, "...neither male nor female; for you are all alone in Christ Jesus" (Gal 3:28). The interpreters differed about her personality:

1. St. Jerome sees that she is a chosen lady, whom the apostle did not mention her name, which is the most common opinion. It is likely the case that St. John did not write her name due to being conservative because she is a lady, or to avoid the annoyances of the Roman Empire.

2. Some say she is "the chosen Kriya," meaning to be the chosen lady, "eklesketa."

3. Some think that her name is "Kiriya"

4. A fourth group notes that Kiriya means lady, and that this is symbolic of a specific church, for she is the chosen bride of Christ. This group interprets "the children of your elect sister" (v.13) as being the children of the Church which St. Paul shepherds

MAIN THEMES AND STRUCTURE
OF THE SECOND EPISTLE OF ST. JOHN

Special Features of the Epistle

This epistle is characterised by the same spirit of St. John who emphasises "the truth" upon which his mission is based, for it declares Christ and "love," for there is no "truth" without love, and there is no true love without "truth," that is Christ. Refer to the first epistle of St. John for the structure of the second epistle.

Introduction to
THE THIRD
EPISTLE OF ST. JOHN

THE SUBJECT OF THE EPISTLE

St. John sent this epistle to Gaius, which is a Greek name for someone. He praised Gaius for his generosity and hospitality for servants.

WHO IS GAIUS?

It is hard to know his personality. This name was often mentioned in the New Testament and was mentioned to be from Corinth (Rom 16:23). Some think that this epistle is directed to him, but this is not certain. It may also have been directed to Gaius from Corinth (1 Cor. 1:14), Gaius from Macedonia (Acts 19:29), or Gaius of Derbe (Acts 20:4).

Introduction to
THE EPISTLE OF
JUDE

THE AUTHOR OF THE EPISTLE

Jude was the brother of James, Bishop of Jerusalem and the writer of the Epistle of James, a cousin of our Lord Jesus (Matt 13:55; Mark 6:3). Jude at first didn't believe in Christ (John 7:3-5), but after His resurrection he became His follower (Acts 1:14).

THE AUDIENCE OF THE EPISTLE

Time and Place of Writing

The epistle was written in 66 or 67 A.D. to warn the Church against false teachers, who had a "Gnostic attitude." They denied the biblical doctrine of creation, for they believed that the creation of the body and material universe is evil and dark. They also denied the true incarnation of Christ. In their opinion, he was not a real man, but he seemed to be so and to have a body. He had an imaginary flesh, or a celestial body, come down from heaven and He was not of St. Mary. The people he was writing to were disobedient to the Church faith, proud, and lovers of money, and were also hypocrites and deceivers. They practiced asceticism to appear as spiritual leaders, whilst simultaneously practising sexual immorality.

PURPOSE OF THE EPISTLE OF ST. JUDE

St. Jude called the believers, "Sanctified ones", who are preserved in Jesus Christ to exhort them to live in sanctity, and to defend the true faith. Sanctity of life and "Truth" are inseparable. What does the verse "You should earnestly contend for the faith which was once delivered unto the saints" mean? The Greek word "epagonizesthai" (contend) means "to fight while standing on a fortress at all costs."

MAIN THEMES AND STRUCTURE OF THE EPISTLE OF ST. JUDE

Special Features of the Epistle:

The meek and sanctified believers have to struggle for the perseverance of the deposit of faith, which we receive through the living tradition (1 Tim. 6:20; 2 Tim. 3:14). Believers have to defend this faith by their godly conduct and by sound doctrines.

St. Jude presents three illustrations from history: God's people in the wilderness, fallen angels, and Gentiles (Sodom and Gomorrah).

Introduction to
THE BOOK OF
REVELATION

IN THE INTRODUCTION TO
THE BOOK OF REVELATION, YOU WILL FIND

About the Author

✳

Purpose of the Epistle

✳

Main themes and structure of the Epistle

✳

Contemplations of the Church and Key
ideas of the Book

THE AUTHOR OF THE BOOK

The early Church unanimously agree that the writer of the Book is St. John the Evangelist. The following points prove this:

1. The writings of the early Church attribute the book to him.

2. He was the apostle considered by the churches of Asia Minor, which is mentioned in the book.

3. History assures us that the Emperor Domitian exiled John the beloved to Patmos Island, where the apostle beheld his revelation (1:9).

4. Although the theme of his book differs from the gospel according to St. John, some common words occur across both books that do not appear in others, such as "the Word, the Lamb, the Victory..." Also, the word 'truth' was repeated in both books.

5. The apostle did not hide his name but mentioned it frankly four times in this book. This is because he is talking about prophecies. In order to trust in them, we need to know the writer in whom God had inspired. However, he did not mention his name in his gospel, nor in the three epistles out of humbleness.

Time and Place of Writing:

This book was written on a small and rocky island which lies about 25 miles far from the shores of Asia Minor (modern Turkey) called Patmos and is now called 'Patino.' It is about 10 miles long and 6 wide, where the apostle wrote this Book during his exile (1:9). Some scholars think that he recorded the revelation he saw in his exile when he returned to Ephesus. There is no proof to support this opinion, however, especially since he was ordered to write what he saw without delay (1:10,11). On this island there is a cave that the inhabitants call the apostle's residence during his exile.

The majority believe that it was written after the destruction of Jerusalem, about the year 95 A.D. St. Irenaeus says that this revelation was proclaimed at the end of Domitian's reign.

THE PURPOSE OF THE BOOK OF REVELATIONS

The Significance of the Book

The Holy Bible began with the Book of Genesis, which proclaimed the endless love of God towards man. He created everything for him, bestowed authority upon him and granted him that much dignity. Yet, the scene soon changed, and the picture was distorted when Man who was living in Paradise was expelled, degraded and bearing upon his shoulders the bitter crime of mutiny. He was afraid to meet with God and escaped from divine justice.

However, by God's grace, He did not leave man to live in this way, aroused by sin. He concluded His Bible by the Book of Revelation, giving us a joyous picture--an open gate in heaven, an eternal Paradise awaiting humanity, divine bosom hastening towards mankind, heavenly harps, joy, and a heavenly wedding for man. What a delightful and splendid book that is appropriate for every believer to hold, keep at heart, meditate on, and constantly repeat day and night. It is the book of hope, victory and praise; it is, in its entirety, the book of heaven.

MAIN THEMES AND STRUCTURE OF THE BOOK OF REVELATIONS

The Book of Hope

Whoever reads the Book of Revelation discovers what the Christian worship is actually about. It is not just duties to be carried out, rituals to be performed, or orders to be observed. One sees through all of this, the invisible divine hands hurrying towards him to receive him, embrace him and raise him up to the heavens where he lives as a partner in the eternal glory.

Whoever tastes the Book of Revelation, no matter how much his fasts are, how long his prayers are, his kneeling, asceticism, depravation, suffering and his everyday crucifixion; they all turn to unspeakable joy and happiness. Through this book, one is dazzled by the love that binds the Creator with His creation, the victorious with the strugglers, and the heavenly with the human. Thus, one forgets about every pain or hardship for the sake of this everlasting love.

The Book of Victory

When the soul enters into the Book of Revelation as a bride visiting her Bridegroom's heaven, she sees a wonderful Paradise and a startling glory prepared to receive her. There, she becomes a friend of the Bridegroom. It is also there that she accompanies His servants, and she falls in love with the heavenly atmosphere of joy and sweetness. At that time, she will not fear the slyness of her enemy "Satan," nor be disturbed by him because she will recognise the power of her Bridegroom, His plans, disposal of evil, and intentions towards her.

The Book of Praise

When the believer spends some time secretly in escape from the outer and inner voices, and enters into calmness and silence with the Bridegroom in the book, he hears hymns of praise and learns the language of unceasing praise. It is beautiful in that the believer does not listen to unknown hymns, but feels that he had learnt it before at his mother's house, "the Church," when he listens to the "hymn of Moses," the "Lamb's hymn" and the hymn of the "Sanctification." These and others, the church trains every heart on, unceasingly, as we shall see.

The Book of Heaven

When the believer forgets all that is around him, he withdraws from amongst the earthly treasures and enters into the Book of Revelation, where the treasures he sees in it dazzle him. He will see heavenly glories that words cannot describe. He will see precious stones, crowns and white robes. Therefore, the heart settles there and refuses to belittle itself again by getting involved in earthly distractions. One will sell all his pearls to acquire the one pearl of great price.

CONTEMPLATIONS OF THE CHURCH AND KEY IDEAS OF THE BOOK OF REVELATIONS

The Church's Contemplations on the Book

In spite of what heretics such as Marcion had stirred up with regards to the canonicity of this book, we find that the Church has given it special care since the early centuries. Therefore, some fathers have explained it and some wrote articles about it, among them being: Justin the Martyr, Irenaeus, Hippolytus8, Melito, Victorinus, Dionysius of Alexandria, Methodios, Basil the Great, Gregory of Naznianzus, Cyril the Great, and Gennadius.

The Difficulty of the Book of Revelation

The interpretation of the Book of Revelation is considered a difficult task for the following reasons:

1. It is a prophetic book (22:7)—It is the only prophetic book in the New Testament.

2. It has prophesies about spiritual heavenly facts that cannot be expressed by human languages, therefore it came in numbers, symbols, colours and similes.

3. It speaks about matters that the faithful do not have to understand the details of. It remains secretive, because if he knows about the times,

he would become lazy and hopeless. Also, if he does not know about the hardships he might face during his struggle, he would also fall victim to despair. The Book of Revelation therefore presents to us the events with the amount that makes the heart burn with fervor and becomes filled with hope without being concerned of the times or even curious to know about future events.

4. Its words bear profound meanings by which the church fathers viewed in amazement.

St. Jerome wrote to Fr. Paulinus, bishop of Nola, saying, "The secrets of the Book of Revelation are as numerous as its words, each word bears a secret. Still, this is little compared to the high honour of this book, that in fact every praise is counted insignificant, because every word carries many meanings. In this book I praise what I understand and what I do not understand."

Pope Dionysius of Alexandria says, "...having formed an idea of it as a composition exceeding my capacity of understanding, I regard it as containing a kind of hidden and wonderful intelligence on the several subjects which come under it. For though I cannot comprehend it, I still suspect that there is some deeper sense underlying the words. And I do not measure or judge its expressions by the standard of my own reason, but, making more allowance for faith, I have simply regarded them too lofty for my comprehension; and I do not forthwith reject what I have not been able to discern its importance."

The Key Points of the Book

In this book, the Holy Spirit accompanies the human soul on the eternal road, revealing to its inner senses how to see, hear, touch and grow stronger until it reaches the eternal wedding.

It begins by showing an "open door in heaven" to ascend to it through our Lord Jesus, the Lamb standing as if slain, ... so what do we see? We first see "the state of the Seven Churches," that reveals the extent of human weakness and how powerful the work of grace is in the Church.

Here, our Lord Jesus comes to announce that He is the only cure to our weaknesses.

Then, He carries the human soul up, as if with a dove's wings, towards eternity on the road of the cross, the road of pain; to see the Lamb opening "the Seven Seals." It proclaims a state of permanent war between God who cares for His children and Satan who never ceases fighting against the children of God.

From there, we hear "the Seven Trumpets," proclaiming God's warnings to mankind in order not to accept Satan's deception, but to be attached to God. They also proclaim the power of the woman clothed with the Sun, against her enemy the sea monster and whoever he arouses: "the sea beast and the land beast."

We will also see the "Seven Strokes" to discipline the wrongdoers, that they might repent; revealing the destruction befalling the adulteress and her lovers. Every time the soul discovers a bitterness that prevails mankind, or a difficulty that encompasses the faithful, we find that our Lord Jesus immediately appears in one way or another to encourage, sympathise, and strengthen His children, in order to accomplish their struggle in peace.

At last, the Spirit accompanies the soul into the "Heavenly Jerusalem", to see and be dazzled by what must be for her sake and what God has planned for mankind, as she watches Satan with her eyes, the enemy of humanity, be thrown down into the lake burning with fire.

www.ingramcontent.com/pod-product-compliance
Lightning Source LLC
Chambersburg PA
CBHW022120080426
42734CB00006B/201